# Anarchy—
# In a Manner of Speaking

T0083502

**ANARCHIES**
Edited by Mehdi Belhaj Kacem and Jean-Luc Nancy

# David Graeber

# Anarchy—
# In a Manner of Speaking

Conversations with
Mehdi Belhaj Kacem, Nika Dubrovsky,
and Assia Turquier-Zauberman

**DIAPHANES**

© DIAPHANES,
ZURICH-PARIS-BERLIN 2020

ISBN 978-3-0358-0226-9

LAYOUT: 2EDIT ZURICH
PRINTED IN GERMANY

WWW.DIAPHANES.COM

# Contents

# A dialogue
# that doesn't cover up its traces

**MEHDI BELHAJ KACEM:** The ANARCHIES collection aims to question the notion of anarchy in the philosophical, scientific, aesthetic, erotic spheres ... but, to question the sphere which perhaps embraces all those which I have just spelled, and which is the political sphere, it seemed to me that there was no better interlocutor in the world than you, David Graeber.

**DAVID GRAEBER:** Questioning the role of anarchy in the political sphere... yes, I like that formulation.

The thing I try to avoid is being interviewed as some kind of authority on anarchy. This isn't just for the obvious reasons; it's also because I don't actually know all that much about the history of anarchist political theory. Sure, I'm broadly familiar with Kropotkin, Bakunin. I've even read some Proudhon. But I'm not a scholar of anarchism in any sense; I'm a scholar who subscribes to anarchist principles and occasionally acts on them, though usually in fairly limited ways. In fact I've largely avoided the books. So if you ask me about the difference between Alexander Berkman's vision of direct democracy and Johann Most's, or for that matter the ethics of Leo Tolstoy versus Martin Buber, frankly, I don't know. I can't tell you.

**MBK:** It's the same with me, but this is an experimental book.

**DG:** I like to think it doesn't matter all that much. A case can certainly be made. Anarchism is very different from Marxism after all; it's not driven by heroic thinkers. You never hear anyone say "I'm a Kropotkinist and you're a Malatestian so I hate you." If anarchists form into sects and decide they hate each other (which of course they often do), it's typically over questions of organization or practice of some kind or another: "You're a platformist and I'm a syndicalist" or an individualist, or council communist or what-have-you. And I do know a bit about anarchist practice since I spent a good chunk of my life participating in groups organized on anarchist principles.

Since we are engaged in a dialogue, here, I thought it might be interesting to take dialogue itself as a theme. A lot of anarchist practice—at least the kind I think of as quintessentially anarchist—revolves around a certain principle of dialogue; there's a lot of attention paid to learning how to make pragmatic, cooperative decisions with people who have fundamentally different understandings of the world, without actually trying to convert them to your particular point of view.

It's always struck me as interesting that in the ancient world, whether in India, China, or Greece, philosophy was written almost exclusively in the form of dialogue (even if it's often the kind of "dialogue" where one guy does 95% of the talking.) Thought, self-reflective consciousness, that which we tend to see as making us truly human—was assumed to be collective (political) or dyadic, but something that almost by definition couldn't be done all by yourself. Or rather, solitary reflection was usually the ultimate goal. The aim of philosophy was, often at least, to cultivate yourself to the point where individual self-consciousness might be possible—and different philosophical schools from Buddhism to stoicism tended to employ different forms of meditation, diet, spiritual exercises as a means of ultimately attaining the status of a sage who really could be a self-conscious individual. But it was only by starting with dialogue that one had any chance of getting there.

For me, that's the most important break Descartes introduces. Christian thought had already been moving away from dialogue. But Descartes completely turns things around by *starting* with the self-conscious individual, and only then asking how that individual can have any kind of communicative relation with anyone else. It's the basis of all subsequent European philosophy but it's also absurd, as neuroscience has shown that the ancients were right: real thought is almost entirely dialogic. Not that cognitive scientists usually say it explicitly, because for some reason they too have a strange mental block on conversation, but they do make clear that what's called the "window of consciousness"— that time during which most of us actually are full self-aware, self-reflective beings—is rare and brief;

it averages around maybe seven seconds. Otherwise you're generally operating on autopilot.

Unless, of course, you're talking to someone else. You can have conversations on autopilot too of course, but if you're really interested and engaged with someone else you can maintain it for hours. The implications of this are profound, even though we rarely seem to acknowledge it: most self-aware thought takes place at exactly the moment when the boundaries of the self are least clear.

**ASSIA TURQUIER-ZAUBERMAN:** ... when it isn't clear whose mind is which.

**DG:** Precisely.

So if there's something I'd like to figure out in this particular conversation, it would be the political implications. Twentieth-century political theory tended to pose the individual versus society ("society" being generally a stand-in for the nation-state), and in the same way the individual mind versus some kind of collective consciousness (whether literally, as in Jung or Durkheim, or in the form of some language-like semiotic code that makes thought possible). But this is ultimately a totalitarian logic. Perhaps this isn't surprising, as the century's politics were haunted by so many different forms of totalitarianism: fascist, Marxist, neoclassical economics... The dialogic approach suggests that most of the really important action takes place somewhere in between: in conversation, or deliberation. Yet such conversations have a notorious tendency to cover up their traces. Would it be possible instead to have a conversation that itself exemplifies the very thing we're trying to understand?

**MBK:** I like this idea of dialogue, which pushes our interview a little into abyss. And since when have you been an anarchist?

**DG:** Oh, I don't know. Since I was a teenager I guess. When people ask me why I became an anarchist, I always say that most people don't think anarchism is a bad idea; they think it's crazy. "So you're saying everyone should just cooperate for the common good without chains of command or prisons or police? That's lovely. Dream on. It would never work." But I was never brought up to think anarchism was crazy. My father fought with the International Brigades in Spain. He was in the ambulance corps based in Benacasim just outside Barcelona so he got to observe for himself how a city organized on anarchist principles could work. And it worked just fine. He himself never quite got to the point of calling himself an anarchist—largely because it was only towards the end of his life that he really fully rejected Marxism. But by then he was no longer politically active, so calling himself an anarchist seemed a bit pretentious—but I grew up in a household where anarchism was definitely not seen as crazy. It was treated as a legitimate political position. And if so, what reason is there *not* to be one?

## Introduction to anarchy—
## all the things it is not

**MBK:** There's a generic definition of anarchy in a very important book for us at diaphanes, by Reiner Schurmann, called *The Principle of Anarchy*, which is an oxymoron. It's a counterintuitive definition because it isn't political but historical. It's the period—our period for two centuries—that hasn't had a referent: like the One for the Greeks, Nature for the Romans, God for the Middle Ages or the Self/Consciousness for a modern. It's the principle of the absence of principle, where as you try to hang on to principles they escape you. So we are in anarchy, in a certain sense. Anarchy in art, anarchy in sex and love, and of course in politics. So what is the significance of the appearance of anarchy in the 19th century?

**DG:** So you're suggesting that the fact that anarchism emerges as a political philosophy around the same time as Nietzsche is not a coincidence?

I'd never really thought about this before, but I suppose ... well, thinking about what happened after 1917 and after 1968, both years of world revolution, I once came up with the notion of "flame-out." Basically this refers to what happens when a grand tradition suddenly explodes and runs through every possible formal permutation in a very short period of time. So after 1917 you have Dada, suprematism, constructivism, surrealism. Everything from white-on-white paintings and urinals as sculptures to nonsense poems designed to foment riots shows where everyone is given a hammer and encouraged to smash anything they dislike. After a few years they had exhausted just about any way that formal radicalism could also be politically radical, so there was nothing left. After that an artist could be formally radical and politically conservative (like Warhol) or formally conservative and politically radical (like say Diego Rivera) or even politically radical and just not do art (like the situationists), but that was about it. I think that after the world revolution of 1968 something similar happened to continental philosophy. Over the course of just a few years, philosophers explored almost every formally radical stance you *could* take that had politically radical implications (man does not exist! truth is violence!), leaving it very difficult for radical thinkers to do anything but refer back to them, just as we keep referring back to the post-World War I artistic avant-garde.

So what you're suggesting is that something similar happened with politics itself after the revolutions of 1848. Though in this case, I guess, it would be that every possible modern political position appears simultaneously, from socialism to liberalism to fascism, and we haven't had any really new ones since. Actually it kind of works, since the term "anarchist" was coined by Proudhon in exactly that context. He has someone demanding to know what he was, a republican? A monarchist? A democrat? And finally he says "No I reject all these, I'm an anarchist!" So that might work. But I'm not sure it's an exact analogy.

"Anarchy" as opposed to "anarchism" only really comes into usage later, in the 20th century, at least in English, with anarchists trying to move away from any sense that they were an ideology similar to socialism, liberalism, conservativism, and the rest. They had a point. Socialists aren't really advocates of sociality, liberals of liberality, conservatives of conservation… or certainly not primarily! In a sense, again, it's a way of pointing out that for most political philosophies, the unity of theory and practice is largely true in theory, not in practice. For anarchists it was much more real. But the question of whether that meant the embrace of that sense of fracture and destabilization that capitalism seemed to introduce—in the way that, say, Dadaists and surrealists embraced the chaos and scrambling of old verities introduced by capitalist markets as an anarchic force which would eventually consume capitalism itself… Well, I'm not so sure of that. As far as I'm aware that's more an avant-garde impulse that was usually more aligned with socialism, much in the way Marx in the *Communist Manifesto* praises the bourgeoisie as revolutionary and says we must now complete their work.

But as a result you're always left with a conceptual puzzle: Is the history of anarchism a history of the *word*, or of some generic political orientation or even attitude one believes the word to have come to stand for, but that could exist under many names, even, among people who reject the label "anarchist"? It's a bit like the word "democracy" that way. A lot of people who call themselves democrats don't seem much interested in the practice (at least as I'd define it); a lot of people who live by the practice don't call themselves democrats.

Part of the problem is that our paradigm for a radical social movement is Marxism, and it's very easy to treat the history of Marxism as a series of intellectual discoveries and developments because that's the way Marxists think of it themselves. But anarchists don't really do that. In a way they're at the opposite pole of the spectrum of possibilities. Take the way they divide themselves up internally. Marxist factions are almost invariably assembled around great thinkers arguing with each other over points of doctrine, definitions of reality, whereas anarchists...

**MBK:** ... act.

**DG:** Yes, or at the very least argue about how they *should* act. When anarchists form factions they tend to divide over forms of organization or ethical questions about action—is it okay to break a window? Is it okay to assassinate a government official? Which means that Marxism and anarchism are potentially reconcilable, of course, since if Marxism is a mode of theoretical analysis, and anarchism an ethics of practice, there's really no reason you can't subscribe to both.

Myself, the closest I've come to a definition was to say that anarchy isn't an attitude, isn't a vision, isn't even a set of practices; it's a process of moving back and forth between the three. When members of a group of people object to some form of domination, and that causes them to imagine a world without it, and that in turn causes them to reexamine and change their relations with each other ... that's anarchy, whether or not you decide to pin a name on it and whatever that name may be.

**MBK:** It's the idea of "free association," as Marx put it. But there are some differences between what communists call free association and the original anarchist idea. Can we read the history of the past centuries as a recuperation of anarchist facts by communist ideology? Perhaps it starts with the argument between Marx and Bakunin in the first International Association of Workers.

**DG:** Yes. It's so obvious, if you look at the details, that while Marx ran circles around Bakunin theoretically, it was Bakunin's predictions that all came true. Bakunin was right about which classes would really make the revolutions, about what a "dictatorship of the proletariat" would really be like. Later Marxist commentators typically dismiss Bakunin, often quite contemptuously, by saying he *shouldn't* have got it right, but they really have very little explanation for why he did. As someone who has spent a little time on barricades—not nearly so many as Bakunin, obviously, but more than most intellectuals certainly—I think I can understand that. You get a very intimate sense of the pulse of revolutionary practice, which then as now was very much anarchist in spirit; if you try to put it into words, it usually ends up sounding crude and naive. But ultimately it's grounded in a very sophisticated understanding.

**MBK:** But when Badiou, Žižek, Rancière and so on speak about La Commune de Paris, the word anarchy is never used, when 80% of them were anarchist workers. After that, with the Bolshevik revolution— a recuperation of the Soviets by Bolsheviks—you have the elimination of anarchy by the Red Army, etc. Can we read whole story of political emancipation of the two last centuries as a recuperation, like a hypostasis, in communist ideology?

**DG:** I'm not sure "recuperation" is the word I'd use, more cooptation, but yes, perhaps that's why so many Marxists seem so indignant about the very existence of anarchists.

I remember being very impressed as a teenager when I read somewhere that if you look at the very early 20th century in countries like Spain or Italy, where half of the labor unions were anarchists and half were socialist, the biggest difference was that the socialist demands always focused on more wages and the anarchist, on less hours. One was saying "We want a consumer society for everyone, but we want a bigger share (oh yes and we also want it to be self managed)"; the other wanted out of the system entirely.

Marx insisted it was the most "advanced" sector of the proletariat who would make the revolution; Bakunin said it would be peasants, craftspeople, and recently proletarianized peasants, craftspeople—people who had not completely forgotten the spirit of autonomous production. Of course Bakunin was right: successful revolutions occurred in Russia, Spain, China, not in England or Germany. (You still see that same kind of thinking today with Marxists like Negri, who in the 90s insisted it had to be computer geeks who would kick off the next global uprising, since of course they were the most advanced sector of the proletariat, and ended up having to explain why it turned out to be peasants in Chiapas—admittedly with the help of computer geeks, but the geeks turned out to be mainly anarchists.) So you end up with anarchist constituencies making revolutions, and ending up with socialists ruling them. But—I always point this out—if you look at state socialist system, they claim that they were trying to achieve a consumer utopia as their ultimate aim (which they didn't do very well), but what they did give people was more *time*. You couldn't get fired from you job. So people wouldn't show up, or they'd develop an extraordinarily leisurely style of working: as a Yugoslav friend described to me, you wake up, you buy a newspaper, you go to work, you read the paper... This was an extraordinary social benefit. If you think about it, these were countries that many of them took themselves from impoverished outliers to world powers, even putting people in outer space, all while working four-to-five-hour days! But the rulers couldn't acknowledge that as a social benefit. They had to pretend they were a problem, the "problem of absenteeism." In other words they provided anarchist social benefits to largely anarchist constituencies, then couldn't take credit for it.

**MBK:** Perhaps the difference then is the concept of work value. In communist ideology, there is a sanctification of work.

**DG:** Exactly that. Also, how work is defined: as "production." I've been thinking about that a great deal lately. I've made the argument in *Bullshit Jobs* that the key problem with the Marxist theory that became popular common sense in the 19th century is that the labor theory of value was entirely based on an essentially theological notion of production. If you go back to Hesiod, or to Genesis, it's always the same idea: God is conceived as a creator. We are punished for our rebellion against God by having to imitate him in the most painful way possible. "You want to be like God and make things, create your own life?" Zeus says, or Jehovah, "Fine have it your way. Let's see how well you like it!" It's also a very gendered idea. In Genesis, God curses Adam to produce food through pain and Eve to increase the pain of childbirth; in English we even use the word "labor" for the pain of childbirth. In either case... well, the word production comes from a Latin verb meaning "to push out": so the image seems to be that just as women push out babies fully formed, factories are a kind of male imitation of childbirth, these black boxes shoving things out. You don't really know what happens inside, except the whole thing is terribly difficult and painful. So that's our conception of work. The painful and mysterious creation of objects. Carlyle actually suggested said God left the world perhaps 20% unfinished, just to give us a chance to share his divinity by allowing us to do the rest.

**MBK:** Sometimes I think that God is the result of the all that work.

**ATZ:** Or in the Kabbalah, one of the readings of the creation is that God created the world so as to be able to embrace himself: the urge to produce, to "push out", so that you have some proof of your insides and can enjoy yourself in their extension.

**DG:** Oh that's interesting. Assia's version is actually kind of the opposite of Mehdi's, isn't it? If I have it right (tell me if I don't), Mehdi is arguing that just as what he calls techno-mimetic appropriation creates scientific abstraction, which we then see as an autonomous sphere that generates the very things from which it's abstracted, well... the process creates the idea of God, but the only logical end-point, the telos motivating the whole thing, would have to be the *actual* creation of God, in the sense of an omniscient, all-powerful being. And indeed that's exactly what Silicon Valley and its rivals seem to be up to.

**MBK:** The idea is that technology *is* God. More exactly, if we compare the *concept* we have always given of God to the state of advancement of modern technology, we find that the two now coincide : we speak of an omniscient entity, omnipotent, indestructible... all the predicates that theology and classical metaphysics attributed to God are, at least virtually, realized by modern technology. The transhumanists, in their very stupidity, are right; they only repeat aloud what metaphysics has always announced, as in Leibniz, who considers God as a super-computer, exactly like transhumanists do.

**DG:** Ah, so it's more like the scattered bits of God we're created so far will ultimately be patched together.

The problem for me is... this God as singularity would still not be able to actually *experience* anything, would he? Nika and I were talking about this with Bifo the other day. He's fascinated with the idea that artificial intelligence will finally make it possible to completely separate intelligence and consciousness, since AI would be pure instrumental reason without self-awareness, which I assumed to include inability to experience qualia (qualities, like the color blue)... to which I noted that neuroscientists seem to agree that without emotion, reason would be impossible. People with flat affect due to brain injuries turn out to be incredibly bad at problem-solving as well. So it's as if Descartes posited a totally imaginary break between thinking and feeling, but now we're trying to make it real by creating a God that really would just think and experience nothing.

Assia's Kabalistic God on the other hand seems to be the precise reverse, no? He starts where the other God ends: as total knowledge, power, capacity, but as a result incapable of experiencing anything. But he must be omniscient or else how could he know that? I guess it's this line of thinking that culminates in Whitehead's God, who experiences everything, and is constantly transformed by it, or if you want to turn to anthropology, the way Godfrey Leinhardt describes the Dinka conception of the divine as an endless refraction of experience. The ultimate manifestation of God for the Dinka, he says, is the experience of fellowship that people feel at a ritual sacrifice.

But we were supposed to be talking about anarchy. Now we're talking about God! That feels a little like jumping ahead.

**Nika Dubrovsky:** Not necessarily.

**DG:** Why not?

**ND:** Can you tell me more about the Dinka?

**DG:** They're a Nilotic pastoral people from South Sudan—actually the language they speak is very distantly related to Hebrew, and they're often represented as the closest we're likely to directly observe to the society of the Biblical patriarchs. They have a single God, but endlessly refracted through various sorts of extraordinary experience. But the ultimate experience of God as unity comes after you sacrifice an ox. Everyone has to confess their sins and resolve their quarrels, at least temporarily, and there's an act of bloody violence, but afterwards the experience of common joy and fellowship as everyone settles into the feast, and it's as if the primordial division of the universe between heaven and earth, born of original sin, is temporarily done away with. And that experience, Leinhardt suggests, is God.

**ND:** Then to me, that sounds like for the Dinka, God *is* anarchy. A moment of pure receptiveness, a utopia of amicable communication. It's really the opposite of the singularity, which is an entirely asocial God, a denial of all social reality.

**DG:** ... which is maybe why we have this instinctual fear that it'll turn into Skynet and kill us.

**MBK:** But do continue.

**DG:** Okay, so anarchy. I think it's easy to confuse different meanings of anarchism. Malatesta has this famous complaint. He says, since people are so insistent that a lack of a coercive legal system can only lead to violent chaos, and that therefore anarchists must be advocates of violent chaos, people who actually are advocates of violent chaos start calling themselves "anarchists," which tends to create confusion.

It's probably not true, but people say that the famous symbol of the A and the O is from Proudhon. It would be the letter O, not a circle, and refers to a quote from Proudhon: "Anarchy is order, government is civil war."

**MBK:** Elisee Reclus said, although perhaps it's not him, that anarchy is the maximum of order.

**DG:** I also think that people confuse anarchy with extreme relativism, or philosophical anti-foundationalism, which always makes me a bit nervous. This is why I'm slightly uneasy when I encounter arguments like Schurmann's. Does philosophical anarchy also imply political anarchy, or does it just strip you of any basis to say political anarchy would be preferable to anything else? When it comes to total ethical or moral relativism, well, the most relativistic people I've ever met have been cops. I once spent five hours in an arrest bus with about 40 other people in plastic handcuffs and this one police officer kept coming into the bus to argue with us, a guy we came to refer to, not very fondly, as Officer Mindfuck. He would always take an extreme moral relativist position and say "Sure, you think you are driven by a moral imperative higher than the law, but your problem is you think yours is the only possible legitimate point of view." I've seen that a lot of times since: a cop gives an order that's just completely insane, like surrounding you and then ordering you to disperse, you're stupid enough to try to reason with them, they just say "Oh so you think you have it all figured out, don't you? You have all the answers." That or they hit you with a stick. But of course if you are a pure authoritarian, then pure moral relativism makes perfect sense because in the absence of truth there's only the law.

Well, force and law—the same nasty cosmology that gets enshrined in the language of physics. That's why police and criminals ultimately like each other so much; they both inhabit the same universe. Essentially, it's a fascist universe, one in which force and law are the only ontological principles. For me anarchy only makes sense as an attempt to sidestep that entire dialectic.

**MBK:** For me we are inherently fascist because that is the original sin: the identification of the laws of nature.

**DG:** That was the original sin?

**MBK:** Yes. It's the malediction of human beings with their ability to identify the laws of nature, which is to say science. Science allows a regime of hyper-appropriation that cannot be found in any other animal species. My question is perhaps why, as beings that can describe laws of nature and being, we fail to do the same things in politics, in morals, in ethics. The result of knowledge, the result of science, for me is this question: why does the identification of the laws of nature deregulate the relationship between human beings? That is a question for anthropologists.

**ATZ:** You're saying "Anarchy as a result of the deregulation of relations between humans caused by the identification of the laws of nature"?

**DG:** So that the creation of laws creates chaos essentially?

**MBK:** If you want. The big mystery is why the scientific animal can't control his own functioning when he can control the functioning of every other being.

**ATZ:** That isn't true though!

**DG:** I suspect Giambattista Vico had it exactly backwards. He said: "We humans can understand only that which we made ourselves." In fact we can understand everything *but* that which we made ourselves.

**ATZ:** Right, and David you've defined reality as that which continually evades us. Mehdi, you say we control everything we don't create, but I don't think that's true at all. When we do, it's because we have exerted some form of violence over it, and even then we must uphold the violence to remain in control. On a macro view, ecological failure is the result of that. A big reason we were able to control the environment the way we did was by conceiving of it as dead, so in the end it does die. A large part of the mystery for me has to do with this: our ability to violently make the world comply with our conceptions of it, against our inability to sustain micro utopia.

**DG:** Well, if Assia is right, then the reason we can't apply science to human relations in the same way we can to everything else.

**ATZ:** Although a large part of economics is about trying to do just that.

**DG:** … would have to be that there's a limit to the degree of violence we can apply to other human beings, compared with what we can do to rocks or mice or barley. Granted often there's not *much* of a limit. Still, even if you set up a concentration camp, you usually need collaborators, which you don't in the case of mice. It also makes sense that "scientific" management of human behavior, from Taylorism to Amazon, ultimately traces back to navy ships and slave plantations, closed spaces where some people really did have absolute command of violence over others. It's all born of the whip. I've often said, social theory generally consists of stripping away 97% of what's going on in any given situation to expose a 3% that forms of a meaningful pattern, a pattern that you wouldn't have noticed otherwise. There's obviously nothing wrong with that. How else are you ever going to say anything new? The trouble starts the moment such simplified models of reality acquire weapons. When I defined debts as promises that have been perverted by a confluence of math and violence, I was thinking along the same lines. But—and this is one thing I get from your work, Mehdi—it all follows from the original rift between philosophy and tragedy; in order to constitute a world of scientific laws, where the abstractions seem to generate the realities, all that violence has to be denied, but of course it can't really be, it endlessly returns in what seem perverse and terrifying forms.

## Reins on the imagination— the illusion of impossibility

**ATZ:** I wish what I'm about to say helped me see more clearly into that, into this race between abstractions and "the real which manifests itself".

There is a relationship between the organicity of anarchy that you outline and a certain notion of health. In a political sense, this health manifests itself in the energy it takes to demand what you are owed, and having that energy depends on feeling entitled to it. It seems that our ability to make demands has to do with our sense of entitlement.

I was concerned about the sort of entitlements my "generation" was raised into, ones in which objects and laws mediate our relationship to the world.

I'll give you an example: feeling entitled to commercial travel rather than to free movement. If someone who has lived outside of this enclosure of imagination just points out to you "Hey, why shouldn't you get to freely roam the earth?" for example, the logic of border control and payment tolls doesn't dissipate entirely but separates from the very basic level of reality to appear for what it is: an overlaid architecture. But say all the people who have known something other than this stage of the industrial cosmology disappeared. How much would it be naturalized? Could it be forgotten?

It's a peculiar angle but from what I gather of your sensory experience and political analysis of something we can call anarchy, there is something very humane, very *human* about remembering some of our functions out of order, which is to say less in fear of death and decay (since negating death is choosing death now rather than later). It is somewhat lyrical, but could we forget that much? Politically?

There was this magazine from Occupy Wall Street called *Tidal*, and the communiqué moved me to tears. It read: "We don't even know why we are here, we know neither what to expect nor what to demand because we don't know how the world is really supposed to feel, all we know is that we have this spiritual nausea that we haven't been able to speak about with anyone since no one has much time to speak about the soul," and that "If the phantoms of wall street are disturbed by our presence, so much the better, it is time the unreal be exposed for what it is." I was so moved that people spontaneously came together in 2011 just to check "Are you real too? Ok, so I'm real. You are real. Debt isn't. I'm dying because of this concept. Ideas are powerful, but only some of them, so that if I chose to believe and engage with magic for example it'll be denied. Well, fuck you, I'm a witch."

**DG:** Yeah, why not?

You know I'm friends with the people who wrote that—one is from Ramallah and the other from the Punjab. So if nothing else you can't say these are first world problems.

Your own particular generation, in my estimation, has experienced an unparalleled offensive against any sort of sense of being entitled to anything—more or less what you'd expect from older generations that are busy stripping away all the entitlements they themselves took for granted when they were young. But I've noticed they've created a really toxic culture where young people are encouraged to do it to each other. I call it "rights scolding." There's a right-wing and a left-wing version. The first is more direct: "Who do you think you are that you deserve health care? Or a pension? Or equal protection under the law?" But the left version is in a way more insidious; it consists of lecturing people on how they need to "check their privilege" if they feel they deserve anything that some more oppressed person can't have. You're complaining the cops beat you up? In Indonesia they would have killed you! You're complaining you got evicted? You know some people don't have homes to begin with! It's the influence of Puritanism I think. People are slightly surprised when you point out obvious things like "But isn't the problem not that a straight white man has a sense of entitlement, but that a queer black woman *doesn't?*"

Then there's question of what you're taught to think is even possible.

I lived in Madagascar for two years, in an area that was not under state control in any immediate sense. There was a nation state, but after the revolutions of the mid-70s, it had largely given up on the countryside, and rural communities had basically become self-governing. They'd maneuvered themselves into a situation where no one was paying taxes, and police wouldn't go off the paved roads (which were very few). On the other hand they also knew better than to draw attention to all of this; they understood the stupidest thing you could do in such a situation would be to hang out a flag and declare "Aha! We're independent now!" If they had, people with guns would eventually have had to show up to reestablish state authority.

So rural people in that part of Madagascar, being extraordinarily commonsensical, realized that as long as you pretend the state is there, you could get away with almost entirely ignoring it. They would even come into town periodically to fill out forms and pretend to register things, and the officials in the offices understood they'd be treated with great respect as long as they stayed in their offices, but if they tried to actually exercise their authority, they'd be made utterly miserable with every conceivable sort of passive resistance. And generally speaking they did, indeed, play along.

So by sheer coincidence I am one of the few anarchists I know who actually had an opportunity to witness self-organized communities that existed largely outside of any top-down coordinating authority. They could do it in part just because they didn't put it in such terms. Non-violent resistance, conflict resolution, consensus decision-making, all that was just life; it was the way people had conducted themselves since they were children.

Then some years later, I was back in America and I got involved in direct action groups who were attempting to rebuild these kinds of processes and sensibilities. It took me a while to figure out we were trying to create exactly the same thing. But we had no idea what we were doing, so everything had to be made explicit. Americans pride themselves on being a democratic society, but if you ask the average American "When was the last time you were part of a group of more than five people who made a collective decision on a more or less equal basis?" most will just scratch their heads. Maybe when ordering a pizza. Or deciding what movie to go to. But otherwise basically never.

When I got involved in the Direct Action Network and other anarchist groups, we had regular trainings on how to make decisions by consensus process, and they helped me finally understand a lot of what I'd observed in Madagascar. "Oh, that was a block!" Because in Madagascar all this was so fully integrated in everyday existence, which I guess is the sense you are talking about, Assia. It was a social capacity everyone has that had come to seem entirely unreal to Americans.

But it's more than just never having had the experience of coming to collective decisions. We're also taught such things are impossible. Not directly of course, or not usually. There are endless institutions operating in ostensibly "democratic" societies which might as well have been designed (and in some cases, I suspect, were in fact designed) to teach us that democracy would never really work. We are surrounded by them at all time. Consider the highway system. Taking a train or bus brings out one sort of behaviour. Being behind the wheel of a car brings out quite another. There's a reason, I think, that both the US and the Nazis so self-consciously favored automobile culture over public transportation: it reinforces a certain sense of human "nature."

In many ways the Romans were the political geniuses of the ancient world because they managed to convince so many people, many of whom had long histories of democratic decision-making, that democracy would be a terrible idea. Authors like Thucydides merely propagandized against democracy. The Romans made it visceral. Think of it this way: in ancient Athens you had the Agora, which may have often been quite rowdy but ultimately made collective decisions about the common good. As a Roman citizen the only experience you really had of collective decision-making was in the circus when you put thumbs up or thumbs down to decide whether you're going to cut some gladiator's throat. These games were in fact sponsored by members of the senatorial elite who served as magistrates, and Rome justified its power largely by claiming to impose an even-handed system of rational law. But these same magistrates organized forms of entertainment designed to turn crowds into a lynch mob, to whip up mad passions, alternations of blood-lust and random acts of magnificent generosity, factionalism, idol-worship, scapegoating—all of it designed to convince participants that democracy itself would be a disaster. Let's confine it to the games and let the professionals take care of law and governance. This was extraordinarily effective. If you look at how Europeans—literate Europeans anyway—talked about democracy for the next 2,000 years, they invariably invoked the Roman circus. "We can't have that! The people are a great beast! We've seen how they behave. They'd turn into lynch mobs like the circus."

Actually, if you think about it, that's probably the reason why even today in most "democracies" the criminal justice system is still the least democratic branch of government. Juries, which are chosen by sortition, are the closest we still have to the kind of deliberative bodies common in ancient democracies. But their powers are sharply circumscribed. They can only judge facts, not render judgments; punishment must be meted out by magistrates. Because we can't have ordinary people do that; they'd turn into lynch mobs like the Roman circus. Even very liberally minded people, who claim to be absolutely devoted to democracy, will just automatically assume this.

Obviously lynch mobs have done many terrible things, but so have magistrates. In fact judges have been responsible for far more atrocities than lynch mobs ever have. But do you ever see anyone point to them and say "Well obviously we'll have to abolish judges."

So institutions like the Roman circus, and there are others like it…call them examples of the ugly-mirror phenomenon: experience is organized in such a way as to constantly suggest you are a bad person incapable of coming to term with others in any sort of reasonable fashion.

So here I am back in the US, taking part in anarchist groups that operate on consensus process, taking part in spokescouncils where a thousand people organized into affinity groups, with some basic training in direct democracy—hand-signals and the like—all sit in a room and come to collective decisions without a leadership structure.

Then you walk out of the room and you realize, wait a minute, I've been taught my entire life, in a thousand subtle and not-so-subtle ways, that something like what I just witnessed could never happen.

So you start to wonder how many other impossible things are not really impossible after all? I know the authors of that *Tidal* article experienced that. I think it might be what they had in the backs of their minds.

## Revolutions in common sense

**ATZ:** This brings us back to Clastres' counter-power, which David writes about in *Fragments of an Anarchist Anthropology*: the idea that acephalous societies are not passively stateless but actively and voluntarily so. You write that counter-power not only opposes existing structures of power but also latent possibilities of it. This is important in revealing the voluntarism of non-coercive social organization, that everyone is aware of the possibility of domination but that some have taken measures to prevent it. You give examples of the Tiv or the Piaroa, who live a pacifist life balanced by a cosmos of invisible wars with spirits and such. I wonder whether we couldn't draw a parallel between this agitated cosmos/peaceful life and the "liberté egalité fraternité" rhetoric/"ugly-mirror" experience we have.

**DG:** Ah, so you're saying, while they are constantly reminding themselves of the dangers of authoritarianism, we're constantly reminding ourselves of the dangers of freedom?

**ATZ:** Yes, something like that. They consciously create arenas for aggression in the invisible world so as to seclude the antagonism in the collective sphere. There, it can be worked out by ritual means. Whereas we construct an invisible world of peaceful coexistence—our rituals assert our unity—but our material structures are conducive to competition and individual strife.

**MBK:** There is an American anarchist, I don't remember his name, who said "Equality without freedom, is prison; freedom without equality, is the jungle." It's my central question in politics: what is the best regime for a livable equilibrium between equality and freedom? In my work the path to an answer is through games, which we will talk about later.

We have to talk about the Gilets Jaunes, because although formally there is no reference to anarchy it seems to be in their DNA, like the realization of a lot of anarchist situationist principles. Gilets Jaunes frequently use the expression of "collective brain," and they refuse vertical power.

**DG:** Excellent! That was my intuition, I know some people on the ZAD, and there was originally a statement made about creating popular assemblies and horizontalism. I wrote something essentially saying that this would emerge and I hoped it was true. I wasn't using the terminology of the event when I was formulating this but more of Immanuel Wallerstein's idea of world revolutions. I actually knew Wallerstein. He was at Yale when I was; we became friends, and I was quite impressed by his thinking in this area. Apparently it all traces back to an argument he had with someone about the impact of the French Revolution. The other fellow argued that revolutions don't make as much difference as we think. Certainly France changed a great deal between 1750 and 1850, but so did Denmark, and they never had a revolution of any kind. Wallerstein made the obvious point that Denmark did have a revolution: the French Revolution. All real revolutions are global in their impact. Starting with 1789 there have been a series of world revolutions, 1848, 1917, 1968… some involved seizing power in one country and some did not, but just involved a series of uprisings across the world, from Germany to Mexico, but in either case the effects were global. The most important of these effects was to change political common sense. Wallerstein made the very simple point that if in 1750 you told the average educated European that "social change is inevitable and good" or that states derive their legitimacy from something called "the people," they'd have probably written you off as some kind of oddball who spends too much time hanging around in cafés. By 1850 everybody, even the stodgiest headmaster, had to at least pretend they agreed with you.

**ATZ:** So when do you think we start to have the problem of revolutions, or at least grand re-calibrations in political common sense, not being followed by any kind of structural change? Yes there was a revolution of principle in 1968, or even after Occupy Wall Street people now know that money doesn't exist, or with the GJ people coming to see—regardless of their opinions—that the violence seen on TV is only a fraction of the violence of the state.

But what of that recalibration in common sense if there is no change at all in the way the power is distributed?

**DG:** Wallerstein would say often the effects are delayed: 1848 was realized in the Paris commune; 1968 was realized in the collapse of the Berlin Wall. Also, often the effects are quite different than one might anticipate. Hence the argument they always make that it was the Russian Revolution that caused the American welfare state.

**MBK:** So-called revolution.

**ATZ:** … and so-called welfare!

**DG:** And you know they say that the Apollo moon landing was the greatest historical achievement of Soviet communism! *[all laugh]*

**ND:** All this was an acute irony for us on the other side of the Iron Curtain. Here we were with our hammers and sickles, but without toilet paper or sausages, and the result was that the capitalists showered workers in France or America with benefits so they wouldn't come over to our side. Then of course the moment we put the hammers and sickles down, because we thought we'd get some of those benefits too, what did they actually do? Take away yours too.

**DG:** So of course when 2011 happened I emailed Wallerstein and asked him whether he was talking about a world revolution of 2011, and he said "absolutely." So the question is, what was the transformation of common sense that was affected by these particular events—the Arab Spring, the squares movements, Occupy? I think it changed our fundamental assumptions of what a democratic movement would have to be like. Democracy is now seen to be largely incompatible with the state. This is precisely why it makes sense for the Gilets Jaunes to be anarchists! And there is also a generational change, which I find extraordinary. If I am not mistaken, a majority of Americans under the age of 30 now consider themselves anti-capitalist. When has that ever happened before? Not in the 30s, not in the 60s. This is a genuinely profound transformation!

**MBK:** And for you that was Occupy Wall Street?

**DG:** Yeah, I guess it worked.

**MBK:** Still, the only revolution that has had long-term universal effects is the French Revolution, through human rights. You're right, though, that whenever a major political event occurs, its effects are global.

### Feminist ethics in anarchy— working with incommensurable perspectives

**MBK:** Historically, feminism is very important in anarchy, whereas in communism—if you scratch beneath the surface—you find good old-fashioned machismo. There's a contradiction between political idealism and the hypostasis of the worker, and the vision of the mores. Some of the greatest anarchist thinkers were women.

**DG:** Yes, Emma Goldman, Lucy Parsons, Voltairine De Cleyre, Louise Michel, Elizabeth Gurley Flynn...

This is what I was trying to get at earlier when I started talking about "production." Marxism doomed itself by adopting an extremely patriarchal, and yes, I'd agree, macho definition of labor, and that reinforced the macho politics. After all, most work isn't "productive" in any literal sense; it's about nurturing, cleaning, transporting, tending to, repairing, arranging, maintaining things (and not just things, but people, animals, plants...) You "produce" a cup once, you wash it a thousand times. All that gets shunted aside in the classic Marxist formulation, it's discounted as women's work. But that also makes it much more difficult to see women's political contributions as work either. All the social labor, interpretive labor, that's required to make it possible for your male theorist to stand on his soapbox and make grand declarations.

I was very impressed recently reading an essay by the Brazilian anthropologist Carlos Fausto on Amazonian concepts of ownership. Consider a spear. You find a good piece of wood, you shape it into a spear, you use, keep and maintain it. We're used to thinking all the action is in the moment of shaping: the tool should belong to the producer. An Amazonian looks at the first and last stage. you didn't produce the wood. In fact, you seized it through an act of predatory appropriation from the gods (we'd say, "nature"), and yes, you shape it, but after that you take care of the thing. It's the process of turning predatory appropriation into nurturant care that is the paradigm for ownership in Amazonia, he says. Often the metaphor is a game animal, a parrot or agouti, that you don't kill and eat but end up keeping as a pet.

I'm convinced it was this obsession with "production" that ultimately undermined the labor theory of value, which had been almost universally accepted in the 19th century, and allowed capitalists to reverse the terms and say "No, we're the *real* creators of wealth." But as I say it also had political effects. Now, obviously, anarchism has had more than its share of macho jerks as well, but it recognized women's liberation as important from the start. You can't just say yes, yes, after the revolution we'll get to that. Since anarchism is so focused on practice, and since in most radical groups it's the women who do the actual work of organizing and coordinating, it becomes much hard to ignore that. Anarchist process comes as much out of feminism as it does out of political anarchism. Also out of the Quakers, a religious tradition, and partly also through the Quakers from indigenous American traditions as well—both a spiritual practice and a form of feminist practice. What I felt really came from feminism, and specifically from what's called feminist care ethics, is the idea that you start with a concern for the particular, this person, this problem, this landscape or ecosystem we wish to preserve, and then bring in universal principles—reason, justice, non-violence—to support that initial commitment. The general is brought in to serve the purposes of the particular, rather than the particular being seen as generated by generalities.

So in a consensus-based process, you're not attempting to bring people around to a common definition of reality. You start with the assumption that everyone's perspective is to some degree incommensurable. And that's good; that kind of difference is a value in itself. Your unity instead lies in a common commitment to action. Thus if there are formal principles of unity, they won't start, as they do in so many Marxist groups, by laying down definitions—"We define ourselves as friends, or comrades, or the vanguard of the proletariat"—but rather, with purposes, "We want to do this." This is what I find so refreshing about the anarchist sensibility. You don't even want to achieve ideological uniformity. Now, you might object, how can you act with common purpose if you can't even agree on who or what you are? But in practice it's actually not so paradoxical, provided you do agree on what the problem is, what you're trying to do. If you think democracy is problem-solving, well, who's going to be better able to solve a problem? Eight people who are so similar they might as well be clones, or eight people with different experiences and perspectives? Clearly you're going to have more creativity and insight with the latter.

**MBK:** That's the illusion that is shattering now with the Gilets Jaunes. Everyone realizes that all deputies in parliament think the same since they all come from the same milieu, the same schools, etc. They are enemies on paper, but that's it. It's a spectacle, as Debord would say. You give the spectacle of political antagonism, but once they exit the parliament they're all friends.

**DG:** Well put! I guess you could say that parliamentary politics is the precise opposite of democracy (at least democracy in the anarchist sense). In mainstream politics, consensus doesn't really have to be achieved, because really the political class are in almost complete agreement on everything from economic theory to the nature of reality to the possibility and desirability of social change. So politicians can spend their time creating artificial divisions over precisely calibrated "wedge issues," setting fires and putting them out, because ultimately it hardly matters. Anarchists start with groups of people who already live in radically different realities and try to create pragmatic unities, over particular courses of action.

It's only if you see reality as generated from the categories that the issue of incommensurability becomes such a terrible problem. If you think about it, what real politics is, what consensus process is trying to do, is precisely to figure out how to reconcile incommensurable perspectives in a practical situation of action. That's what anarchism is for me: a community of purpose without a community of definition. Politics as currently conceived is the exact opposite of this. We're all supposed to agree on what reality is, and then we fight it out because we lack a common purpose, or have contradictory identities and interests.

**ND:** Coming from a Soviet experience that was not exactly communism, but really more a version of monopolistic capitalism. It was very funny, what we studied in school. We were trained to memorize the definition of communism, but it was something poetic and abstract that didn't mean anything. In practical matters, we were of course expected not to discuss anything deemed too complicated; political theory should only be discussed by people with technical training. It was a contradiction where we weren't allowed to have common action, but had to agree on something that it wasn't possible to agree on since we didn't know exactly what it was.

**DG:** I sometimes call that "mythic communism" or "epic communism." Once upon a time we used to share all things in common. Now everything has gone wrong, but someday we shall attain true communism once again. It's all very messianic, as endless critics have pointed out, but it also makes it very difficult to connect everyday practice to one's ideals. That's why I insist we define communism only as a practice, when people actually interact on the basis of "from each according to their abilities, to each according to their needs." In that sense, we're communist all the time. All societies actually are founded on a certain level of baseline communism (Can you give me a light? the time? In many societies, food ...) or they wouldn't be "societies" at all. And of course if people are working on a common project, they automatically behave communistically because it's obviously the most efficient way to proceed. If I'm fixing a pipe, even if it's for the office of Monsanto, or Goldman Sachs, and I say "Hand me the wrench," the other guy doesn't say "Yeah, and what do I get for that?" He has an ability, I have

a need. We even justify the market on that basis—
"supply and demand" are transpositions of "ability
and need"—to justify capitalist markets we claim
(falsely) that they're really forms of communism.
But forms of cooperation really are communism.
Which means that in a practical sense capitalism is
just a bad way of organizing communism. We don't
need to create communism. We just need to find a
better way of coordinating it.

**ATZ:** I'd like to make a note on how we're using the
terms and how we're circling them. You just rede-
fined the Soviet Union as "monopolistic capitalism," and spoke of capitalism as "badly organized
communism." Maybe that's something to unwind ...

**DG:** You're suggesting, perhaps, that state socialism
is a bad way of organizing capitalism in the same
way as capitalism is a bad way of organizing grass-
roots communism!

**ATZ:** Yes! And maybe this is where we hit the walls
of that particular architecture of imagination. Since
we are on the track of exposing which enclosures
and impossibilities are fabricated by a social structure that feeds off of this gaslighting, I would be
tempted to say that the state is ultimately the problem. Yet I get the impression that you have been
moving away from that position, David.

# The three characteristics of statehood and their independence (two for us, one for the cosmos)

**DG:** Yes, I have.

It may seem odd, because anarchism is traditionally conceived as opposition to the state, but I'm becoming increasingly convinced that when we imagine a state, we're thinking about three different things with entirely separate historical origins that just happen to have come together, and which we have been trying to convince ourselves ever since have some kind of necessary relation to each other even though in fact they don't. On the one hand you have the principle of sovereignty, which is the ability to exercise coercive power over a territory, basically to be as violent as you like with impunity. Then you have the principle of administrative organization, which is about the control of knowledge. And finally you have the existence of a competitive political field. If you look at it historically, it's very easy to find examples in which these things did *not* come together.

Take the divine kingship of the Shilluk—the Shilluk being another Nilotic pastoralist people, much like the Nuer or Dinka, except they have a king. The Shilluk king—or they call him the reth—embodies sovereignty in its purest form. The king can do absolutely anything he likes—when he's physically present. But when he isn't he has no power because he has no bureaucracy whatsoever. There's no principle of administration, and ordinarily there's no competitive political field either, except when the king dies, when there's a yearlong inter-regnum when rival successors vie for power, but after that it disappears again. The king is relegated to this little bubble, a town full of his wives and a few henchmen, and a special bodyguard that will someday execute him when he becomes too old, a town which everyone normally avoids. And when he comes around everybody hides because he can do whatever he wants—grab their daughters, raid their cattle. Otherwise he only shows up to render judgment at trials. Insofar as there is administration, it's mostly his wives, since he has perhaps a hundred of them, and they visit their natal villages periodically. These wives, incidentally, are empowered to collectively order the king's execution when they decide he's too old and weak to satisfy them sexually. The latter is a particularly Shilluk twist, and there's evidence the whole system was set up by a certain Queen Abudok, who was deposed and came up with the rules as a kind of compromise—but the essential pattern is surprisingly common. The Natchez, in what's now Louisiana, seem to have had something almost exactly similar: the king could do or take whatever he wanted when he was there; otherwise people just ignored his orders. Call this sovereignty in the raw.

In Sumer, the first "states" we really know about, they had no principle of sovereignty at all, and therefore no real state in the Weberian sense of an organization that successfully claims a monopoly of coercive force within a given territory. There's nothing even remotely like police, but you do have incredibly complex multi-layered forms of administration.

Similarly, political fields where larger-than-life figures compete over glory and followers... that's not Sumerian either. If anything it's anti-Sumerian. My friend the archaeologist David Wengrow pointed this out. If you look at all the great epic traditions, whether the Rig Veda or the Homeric epics, later the Nordic or Celtic or Balkan epic cycles, they are never about the great civilizations. They're about the barbarians in the hills that warred and traded with the great civilizations. Both the urbanites and the barbarians came to define themselves in opposition to each other. Schismogenetically. So if the Sumerians create a commercial and bureaucratic society, then the barbarians refuse to use money, refuse writing (instead they have priests and poets who extemporize heroic verse or memorize cosmological epics). Where the city people pile up wealth and keep careful count, they have festivals where they dump it in the ocean or set fire to it. But above all the barbarians develop a politics that centers on heroic figures who are constantly competing in games and sacrifices and contests of one sort or another. You could say they were the first politicians. And now we assume that's what democracy is all about, but for most of human history it was considered the very opposite: democracy was collective problem-solving; dramatic public contests between heroic figures was aristocracy.

Greek city-states were descended from Homeric barbarians, living at the fringes of the great civilizations of the Middle East. But gradually they acquire some bits of an administrative state—and they attempt to fuse the two together, heroic politics and bureaucracy—although still without a principle of sovereignty. That gets projected onto the gods.

Actually David Wengrow came up with the interesting theory that most early states have two of the three, and the third gets projected onto the cosmos somehow. The Mayas, for instance, had heroic politics and sovereignty, but bureaucracy was projected into the gods. Egypt had sovereignty and bureaucracy, but politics was projected onto the gods, and so forth.

Still, the key point is that what we think of as "the state" is a conjuncture of three elements that didn't arise together, and historically usually had little if anything to do with one another. And that's why it's so difficult for people to understand what's happening today in terms of globalization, because we have a principle of administration on a global scale but we don't have either a political field or a single overarching principle of sovereignty. The War on Terror tried to create something like that, but it clearly failed.

**MBK:** You often criticize the opposition between market and state in the same way.

**DG:** Yes. That opposition is entirely illusory. Both come out of each other. Markets are created through sovereignty. Impersonal markets and coined money were largely created to provision armies, but markets and administration also follow the same logic of impersonal rationality.

Take in the case of the alter-globalization movement, which was how I first got involved in anarchistic social movements. Why, we were always asked, would an anarchist be opposed to globalization? Well, we weren't opposed to globalization, of course; we were opposed to capitalist globalization, but even if you explained that, then they'd say "Well, if you're against globalized markets, doesn't that mean you're pro-state? You're arguing for the restoration of national sovereignty. How can an anarchist do that?"

But in fact, where they saw "globalized markets" what we saw was a global administrative system—made up of institutions like the IMF, World Bank, WTO, but also transnational corporations, banks, NGOs, credit-rating agencies—that knitted together into something that resembled a global state. Markets don't happen all by themselves. You need all sorts of bureaucracies to create and keep them running.

## America 1— not a democracy, never meant to be

**MBK:** Anarchy for me is asking what is the alternative between freedom without equality and equality without freedom. You say "In the US we have so many laws. It's a very juridical, fanatical country." You have so many TV series about lawyers and cops. The schizophrenia of people being both anti-imperialists watching *NCIS* or *Law and Order*, and the efficiency of American propaganda in the world... How do you explain the fact that the most radical attempts to create a political alternative in USA have been by anarchists and not communists?

**DG:** I think it has to do with the contradiction of the idea of democracy in America. On the one hand,

Americans are always being told they are the world's greatest democracy, and I think most do have a certain democratic spirit, at least in the sense that they don't like being governed very much, and feel that people should govern themselves, however much they might not know what that means. Still, they're also taught to idealize the legal order and the constitution, which creates an enormous contradiction. If you want to annoy a conventional American political thinker, it's quite easy: just point out that there's no place in the US Declaration of Independence or constitution that says anything about American being a democracy. The people who wrote these documents were steadfastly opposed to democracy, and said so all the time. In fact, the very first speech during the Constitutional Convention explicitly said we have a problem; there is a danger of democracy breaking out in this country. So the constitution was explicitly anti-democratic. Mind you, at that time the words "democracy" and "anarchy" were used almost interchangeably. They were both terms of abuse for people who believed in "mob rule," or "mobility," as they sometimes called it.

**ATZ:** Ha! That's really really funny. When you think of the greatest fear of the present system being some kind of.

**DG:** … democracy yeah!

**ATZ:** No but you know, upward "mobility" being the unkept promise of democracy, the poetics of that are really funny.

**DG:** There's a brilliant letter by one of the early patriots, a certain Gouverneur Morris (Gouverneur actually was his first name), who was at the time the largest landowner in New York. They had called out "mobility," the mob, against the authorities over some issue or another, but after the riot the rioters stayed on, and it turned into a debate about what the constitution of an independent America should be like: should it a Roman-type republic or an Athenian-type democracy? People were citing Polybius and making a strong case for a bottom-up system. Morris was horrified. "The mob," he wrote, "begin to think and reason!" Suppressing education obviously wasn't a viable option. He began to conclude that British rule might not so be so bad after all.

Popular assemblies did emerge during the revolution, but they were ultimately suppressed just like the Soviets. Still, there is a kind of popular ideal, or aspiration, very rarely realized in practice, that lingers in America. This is why even though "democracy" was largely used as a term of abuse, the term had an appeal. But the Founding Fathers, as they're called, were very explicit that they wanted Rome, not Athens, as their model. That's why there's a Senate in America.

**MBK:** I didn't know that.

**DG:** The ideal was for a "mixed constitution," like Polybius claimed Rome and Carthage had: the executive would represent the monarchical principle, the Senate, which is the oligarchical principle, and the Congress the democratic principle—though the latter was largely limited to raising and disposing of public funds.

However, even though America is set up as a republic and not as a democracy, by the 1830s Andrew Jackson ran as a democrat and won, and everybody just relabeled republics as democracy. So these institutions that were designed to suppress democracy were relabeled "democracy" and people have been living with this contradiction ever since: that democracy is both the ideal that people should be participating in decisions affecting their own lives and a set of institutions which were designed to make that as difficult as possible. All American social movements work themselves out through that tension.

**ND:** The Soviet Union was called "Soviet" because it literally means "council," as in general assembly. And a year after the revolution they dismantled it and left nothing but the name, which is exactly the same. These countries are so similar.

**DG:** Absolutely. Then the question that I always find interesting is why people like the idea of democracy so much despite the fact that no one said anything good about it! What was it they saw?

**ATZ:** And so?

**DG:** I think that's what we're here to try to figure out.

# America 2—the indigenous critique & freedom works fine but it's a terrible idea & Lewis Henry Morgan invents anthropology because he's nostalgic & Americans are legal fanatics because of their broken relationship to the land, which they stole

**DG:** Well, all right, there were a lot of factors in the American case. One is clearly Native American influence, which is unacknowledged but very strong from very early on. A lot of the Puritan fathers were very angry about this, and wrote about it in the early colonies. They'd notice that parents would stop beating their children and complained of "Indianization," that settlers were slowly adopting indigenous ways of doing things. And of course indigenous societies *did* operate on general assemblies and consensus process.

There was a huge academic and to some degree political debate some years ago, called the "influence debate", which came to focus on whether the US federal system was at least inspired by the Haudenosaunee, the Great Peace of the Six Nations of the Iroquois. The focus on the constitution was just a diversion, though, from the original point, originally made by a group of largely Native American historians, that the adoption of those particular institutional structures was part of a much larger adoption of indigenous ideas of freedom and equality.

It wasn't just settlers. Enlightenment thinkers back in Europe were often quite explicit about where their ideas were coming from as well. When

David Wengrow and I started work on our project together, we started intending to write a book on the origins of social inequality. We soon realized this was a foolish question. Better to be asking why we thought there was something called inequality and why we thought it had an origin. So I started researching the origins of the question of the origins of social inequality.

Rousseau wrote his essay for a contest, put forward by the Académie de Dijon, on the question of "What is the origin of inequality among men and is it in accord with natural law?" So this is 1752 in France, Ancien Régime: no one has so much as walked into a room where they didn't know who outranked who. So why did they assume that inequality had an origin? In the Middle Ages they certainly didn't: everyone assumed Adam outranked Eve, right? I found one survey of medieval literature that found that words like "aequalis" or "inaequalis" simply weren't used in social contexts at all, it just never occurred to anyone to frame things in such terms. "Inequality" only really became a concept in the sixteenth and seventeenth centuries with arguments of the New World and ideas of natural law.

The problem was that legal scholars in Spain and elsewhere had no framework by which to think about people who were neither Christians nor infidels—since the peoples of the New World clearly had never been exposed to Christian ideas at all. So how might it be justified to make war on them? These were serious issues. Pizarro almost got in big legal trouble for killing the Inca king, which the king of Spain didn't take kindly to. So the question became: what rights can human beings be said to have just for being human? The obvious place to look was at the very simplest societies, humanity in the raw as it were, to see if there were any universally recognized rights one could say humans always grant one another, or at least think they should.

A lot of what followed was pure fantasy, but by no means all of it. What eventually transpired was a prolonged conversation in which indigenous perspectives were often taken extremely seriously. If you read the *Jesuit Relations of New France*, and similar accounts—which were very widely read by middle-class families back in Europe—you find is a fairly consistent indigenous critique of French, and by extension European, civilization; but the Miqmac, Algonkians, Wendat Huron don't originally talk about equality at all. Actually neither do the Jesuits. It all starts with an argument about freedom, and also mutual aid, and only gradually turns to questions of equality.

The reason why is that it never occurs to indigenous people at first that having more wealth than someone else would mean that you would have power over them.

**ATZ:** And so how come?

**DG:** How come what?

**ATZ:** How come it didn't occur to them?

**DG:** Mainly I think because it was so far removed from their own experience. The women of one Wendat longhouse might have more maize and beans stockpiled, a man might have more wampum and be considered rich, and that might allow them to feel more important than others in certain contexts, but it wouldn't put them in a situation where he could compel anyone to work for them. The entire society was set up in such a way that no one could tell anybody to do something they didn't want to do. So this was the original critique: "What's wrong with you people? You live in constant fear of your superiors! We just laugh at ours if they get too big for their britches. Also you don't take care of each other, you're hyper-competitive and all talk over each other in conversation, you let people starve." But these were largely seen in terms of individual autonomy as well, since a beggar isn't free in any meaningful sense.

Reading the Jesuit Relations causes a certain intellectual confusion because we're trained to see European observers as representing "the West" and therefore "us" and indigenous Americans as alien and perhaps unknowable Others, but when you read the Jesuits' accounts, it's the indigenous people that are making all the arguments we'd be making today—why shouldn't a woman be able to decide what she wants to do with her own body? Or expounding what was essentially Freudian dream theory to confused Jesuits who believed in angels and devils and messages from God. But it's especially striking as soon as the Jesuits start talking about freedom. Nowadays, of course, no one can say anything bad about freedom—at least in principle. But most people say, well, absolute freedom, anarchism, that would never really work in practice. The Jesuits held exactly the opposite position. They keep writing "These are truly free people, they don't believe in taking orders and are constantly making fun of us because we follow orders … and you'd think it wouldn't work, but actually it works very well. They have no punitive laws, just compensation, but actually, there's a lot less crime here than back at home …"

So in fact it works just fine in practice. But they also insist that freedom is terrible in principle. How are people going to learn the Ten Commandments if they don't even have a concept of command?

These reports however were read avidly back home, and readers often reached very different conclusions. And eventually some free-thinkers made their way to Canada as well. The key figure here is a certain Baron Lahontan, an impoverished noble who joined the army and was sent to Quebec at seventeen, and eventually learned Huron and Algonquian, and insisted that since the Indians were aware of his low opinion of the Jesuits, they told him what they really thought of them as well. By the time Lahontan is in Quebec, in the 1680s and 90s, there were towns like Montreal and New York springing up, and a lot of indigenous Americans had seen them. Many had even traveled to France, so you could say they had enough of an ethnographic understanding of European society to figure out that it was one where differences of wealth could indeed be converted into differences of power. So you start to get people explicitly talking about equality.

So the idea of Native American societies as societies of equals emerges from the dialogic encounter, as a point of contrast. They key figure is a certain Kondiaronk, who is essentially the Wendat statesman put in charge of dealing with the French. He came to speak fluent French along with seven other languages, and all accounts treat him as the most brilliant debater anybody had ever met. Even his enemies would come from miles around to watch him speak, and apparently the governor created a little salon in Montreal where he would argue with him about Christianity, law, and sexual morality. They'd go back and forth for hours, with Kondiaronk taking the position of skeptical rationalist and almost invariably carrying the day. Lahontan apparently took notes. Later Lahontan got himself in some sort of trouble and ended up exiled in Amsterdam, so he wrote up these dialogues in a book that came out, if I remember, in 1704. It became a huge bestseller across Europe. There was a play based on it that ran for almost twenty years in Paris. And every single Enlightenment thinker wrote an imitation, some foreign skeptical rationalist making fun of French society: Voltaire had a half-Huron, Diderot had a Polynesian, so forth and so on.

So Kondiaronk was the first to make a systematic argument for social equality, from a rationalist perspective. He took the position that institutions of repressive law, both religious and legal punitive justice, are only made necessary by the existence of other institutions, like money, which encourage us to engage in the exact sort of behavior those laws are ostensibly designed to suppress. If you eliminated the former you wouldn't need the latter.

**MBK:** What about this legal fanaticism in the United States?

**DG:** Actually, I think it's connected to the same story. Kondiaronk liked to pretend that the Wendat had no laws at all, but by that he meant punitive law. But in a sense, many indigenous American social orders were essentially agreements, like the various confederations, and hence creations of positive law. This had an impact on Enlightenment thinking as well. In 1725, the Osage nation—who very much saw their society as one created through a series of what we'd now call constitutional conventions—sent a delegation to Paris where they apparently met with Montesquieu (he actually writes about them in *The Spirit of the Laws*), and obviously this clicked with classical stories about Solon and Lycurgus, and before long, you have this theory that nations are created by great lawgivers... an idea which is then adopted by the American settler revolutionaries, with the result that the United States is perhaps the only nation in the world which more or less does look like what Montesquieu imagined, one where a nation's character is created by its laws.

An anthropologist called David Schneider wrote a book called *American Kinship* where he pointed that there are two categories of relatives in American English. You have blood relatives and in-laws. Anything that isn't immediate family is a legal relationship. That relation between blood and law is essentially the American cosmology, and in some ways its just a transposition of European categories, but it's also very different because you don't have the same relationship of blood and soil. Nobody goes to Bunker Hill let alone Little Big Horn and says "This is where our ancestors died so this land would be eternally ours." Instead there is a vague sense of historical guilt.

In fact America anthropology is a product of that very discomfort. Lewis Henry Morgan, who later became the first professional anthropologist in America, was originally part of a group of New York law students who had this crazy idea to reinvent the League of the Iroquois. This was the 1830s, when romantic nationalism was sweeping Europe, and a lot of Americans felt particularly left out: "Our landscape too should be full of stories, of epic wars and romances, heroic feats, and it used to be, but now we have no way to know what they were because we killed all those people." They were actually reconstructing Six Nation ritual, conducting initiation ceremonies where the spirit of the dead Indians cursed them for having destroyed them, then passed on their knowledge so at least someone would carry it on. Well, one day Morgan was in the state capital, Albany, in a used book store looking for old texts about Iroquois treaty negotiations to help him reconstruct League ritual, and there is this young man reaching for the same book and he says "Oh why are you interested in that?" And the man answers "My name is Ely Parker, I'm a Seneca sachem. What's your story?" And Morgan effectively said "Wait, you guys aren't all dead?"

Such was the birth of American anthropology.

It's significant that the kids who were trying to reconstruct the League of the Iroquois were all lawyers. They talked about a loss of connection with the land, but they must also have been aware that America itself was born of a great crime, perhaps history's greatest crime—the genocidal destruction of countless human societies, the theft of an entire continent. But at the same time Americans also came to identify with the very people they destroyed, to become more like them in significant ways. "Indians" were always a symbol of liberty: the very first act of the American Revolution, the Boston Tea Party where they threw the British tea into the harbor, refusing the pay taxes on it, they are all dressed up as "Indians." You dress up as Indians when you break the law. But at the same time you desperately insist that it's only law that knits you together as a free people.

**ATZ:** So legal fetish as a way of renouncing and denying a broken relationship to the land?

**DG:** Yes and people often argue that's why there's this strangely irrational identification of America with Israel. Same same.

Let me just finish what I was starting to say about the Enlightenment, though. The obsession with equality becomes a theme in Enlightenment thought. Practically every single philosopher (well, except Rousseau) writes at least one essay imagining European society from the perspective of a naive outsider, and usually one presumed to come from a more egalitarian society. In a way, the "Western gaze", that skeptical rationalist scratching his head at the peculiarity of local customs, isn't originally European at all; it's the gaze of the imaginary outsider on Europe. All this comes to a head with a book by a saloniste named Madame de Graffigny. She wrote a book called *Letters* from a *Peruvian Woman* from the perspective of an imaginary kidnapped Inca princess. It came out in 1747, and was remembered by many in the next century as the first book to propose the idea of the welfare state, or even state socialism (though now it's largely remembered as the first novel with a female protagonist where in the end the heroine doesn't either marry or die). At one point the Inca princess says "Why don't they just do what we do, and just redistribute the wealth?"

A few years later, right around the time the Académie de Dijon is announcing its contest for the best essay on the origins social inequality, she's working on a second edition, and sends a copy to her friend Turgot, saying the editors want me to change it around a little, what are your thoughts? We have his response. Basically he says "Well I don't know, all this stuff about freedom and equality is very appealing, but I think you should have your character realize that there are stages of civilization. Freedom and equality might be appropriate for a society with a relatively undeveloped division of labor, such as hunters or even your Andean farmers, but in our own sophisticated commercial civilization (note this is the 1750s so he doesn't say "industrial"), our prosperity is dependent on giving most of that up."

So Turgot proposes the idea of stages of civilization, which Adam Smith takes up a year or two later! For me this is the smoking gun, as it were. The idea of social evolution is a direct response to the indigenous critique of European society. And Rousseau is quite ingenious here, because what he does is come up with a synthesis of the two. He accepts the indigenous critique and fuses it together with the notion of stages of development. And in doing so, one might say, he effectively invents what we have come to think of as leftist thought.

So we start with the indigenous critique of the lack of freedom in European society, which eventually becomes an argument about equality, which in turn inspires a debate between proto-leftists like Diderot and proto-rightists like Turgot, who basically invent the idea of evolution, that you can categorize people as hunters, pastoralists, farmers, etc, and this determines the broader contours of their society ... largely as a way of putting the cat back in the bag. Rousseau is trying to shock everyone but really he's coming up with a clever compromise. So far so good. Rousseau has earned himself a lot of abuse, particularly in right-wing circles, and most of it is undeserved, but I think he did leave us one particularly toxic legacy. Not the idea of the noble savage, since Rousseau didn't in fact argue that savages were noble. More the idea of the stupid savage, that people in free societies were blissful because they were dumb, and, he insisted, almost completely lacking in imagination. It's really remarkable to contrast this with early Jesuit accounts, let alone descriptions of people like Kondiaronk, where the French observers are complaining at how all these people who had never even heard of Varro or Quintilian can wipe the floor with them in a debate.

This idea of the stupid savage is the really disastrous legacy of Rousseau, and it has haunted us ever since. It gets to the point where you have people writing books like *The Origins and History of Consciousness* arguing that "primitive" peoples, or Homeric characters, weren't even fully awake, they existed in a sort of semi-conscious haze, incapable of reflection. Well of course, everyone still wanders around most of the time in a semi-conscious haze, as I was pointing out earlier; we always have and presumably always will. But at least most people in history were aware that humans are mainly conscious when they are talking to others, which is why they developed all these explicitly dialogic modes of thought.

It's ultimately because of Rousseau, I think, that we've moved from self-consciousness being an individual achievement, to seeing it as a historical achievement, if an ambivalent one.

Similarly, we have the idea that collective self-consciousness only became possible around the time of Rousseau himself. This is something even I had largely taken for granted all my life: that it was only in the eighteenth century people began to propose revolutionary visions as legitimate in their own right. Before that I'd always assumed—and the history I had read seemed to bear me out—if you wanted to revolt against some oppressor and propose a new model for society, you had to either claim you were really trying to restore the "ancient ways" that had been corrupted, or else that you had a vision from God. What the Enlightenment supposedly introduced was the idea that you could simply propose a more reasonable way to arrange things, and then try to bring it about, for no reason other than that it was more reasonable. Now this is not true at all, as my earlier remarks about the Osage and Lycurgus already make clear. The idea of giving power to the imagination, as it were, was hardly invented by Rousseau! Rather, what he really did was convince us that "non-Western peoples," as they came to be called, were incapable of imagining anything.

**ATZ:** That makes me think of the piece you wrote: "Culture as Creative Refusal."

**DG:** Ah so you see where I was going with this. Yes. I've always been intrigued by the idea that what we call "cultures" could just as easily be seen as social movements that were actually successful. In other words, no, we don't have to spend our time arguing about Kronstadt for the rest of history, there are innumerable examples of successful revolutions right before our eyes.

## With great responsibility comes precarious tongue-tied intellectuals

**ATZ:** On a linguistic note, that part of your book said that "Clastres and Mauss *laissent voir* this and that"—they allow something to be seen. This struck me as a wonderful phrasing to identify what it is writers do when they do it well, and a much more interesting understanding of what kind of transmission it is: they remind you of something you already know.

**MBK:** Reiner Schürmann says there are two forms of philosophers, those that make visible the invisible, like Plato saying that there are ideas behind things, and those that allow us to see the visible differently.

**ATZ:** Does that have something to do with the relationship between anthropology and economics do you think?

**DG:** That would be the flattering interpretation, certainly. "We are the greatest threat to the hegemonic discipline of our time, because we are the ones who demonstrate that their universal principles of human behavior have no predictive power whatsoever, unless you're dealing with people who've grown up in institutional contexts entirely shaped by the teachings of economics. We had to be neutralized!" Actually it's such a flattering interpretation I'm almost afraid to embrace it. Back in the 80s, when the first movement to neutralize anthropology began (largely from within the discipline itself), it certainly didn't seem that way.

What happened in anthropology—I know the Anglophone world best of course, and especially America—was that there was a kind of a self-questioning in the 80s, a "post-modern moment," as anthropologists called it. This has to do with the fact that American anthropology was always very textual; they sort of rediscovered hermeneutics in the 50s and 60s.

American anthropology comes very much out of the German intellectual tradition, whereas British anthropology pulls on French: Durkheim and then Levi-Strauss. In America it was first Boas, a German, who sort of established cultural anthropology, culture being of course a German concept. Norbert Elias made a famous argument that the reason France came up with the universalistic notion of "civilization" in the 18th century, and Germany came up with "culture," was essentially the different positions of the middle class. In France the emerging bourgeoisie was incorporated into the structure of state and the aristocracy, and they were politically and economically active, so you have this expansive conception of civilization including everything in human life that can be improved, from technology to table manners, and of course the endless salons and forums for debate. So the favored prose style reflected that; it was witty but transparent and conversational. Meanwhile in Germany you have dozens of tiny principalities, in which the aristocracy speak French and the professional classes are frozen out of politics. They mostly never even meet each other, so all they have is shared language and literature; everything is conveyed through texts. National unity had to be created in the imaginary, both as a collective project and as a sort of shared structure of feeling. And of course German philosophy comes up with endless theories of action, and theories of texts as forms of action.

It might seem odd that American anthropology comes to adopt this tradition, considering that the US middle class is positioned a lot more like the French one, but of course US anthropology is not about middle-class folk. It's mainly about understanding indigenous genocide survivors. So in many cases texts are all you've got. After World War II there's a kind of second wave of Germany theory that hits the US academy: Schleiermacher, Dilthey, Weber. Weber is being promoted as the Free World's answer to Marx. In anthropology the great impresario in all this is this character named Clifford Geertz, a archetypal Cold War liberal—his original fieldwork in Java and Bali was literally funded by the CIA—who coins the notion of "culture as text." It's enormously influential. But it's never exactly clear what it means. Since the moment you propose that a Balinese cockfight or gamelan performance or inheritance dispute should be considered a "text," a "story they tell about themselves" as Geertz put it, the obvious question is who's exactly is the "they" being referred to? The Balinese? Balinese culture? In the hermeneutic tradition the author is always something of an abstraction created by the reader, so that's not a problem, but when you create "Shakespeare" in your mind while reading Hamlet, it's as an authorial intention, the meaning of a text is the author's project that unites all the pieces. Fine, but you can't treat "Balinese culture" as an author in that sense. Balinese culture doesn't have a single project; it doesn't mean anything—for Balinese people, at least, it means every possible thing. So the easiest solution is to say that Balinese culture doesn't exist at all; it's just something the ethnographer made up. There is no "author," or rather it's the ethnographer who is taking a pencil, drawing a circle around some imagined totality, and then claiming the hypostasized entity they've just invented is somehow writing the text.

Now in the 60s and 70s there was just beginning to be an internal critique of anthropology, starting from the historical entanglement of the discipline with colonialism, racism, empire—much of it framed in Marxist and feminist terms. But in the 80s, as campus unrest died down, it all settled into an obsession with unmasking the power relation that lay behind the creation of the authority of ethnographic texts. This is of course an entirely legitimate project, but it was sharply limited. Literary criticism was deployed as an ostensibly radical deconstructive tool, but then somehow it was only applied to one stage of the construction of ethnographic texts—the moment when the anthropologist is in the field, and he has all the power. So if I'm in Madagascar, as a rich white guy, well, we analyze what happens there. But what happens when I go back to the US and I'm an impoverished grad student with my teeth falling out because since I'm not from the bourgeois background I'm assumed to be from, I'm working two jobs but still can't afford dental care, and I'm terrified I'll say something wrong and my advisors won't write me a good letter of recommendation and I'll be a starving adjunct for the rest of my life, that is, the time I'm *actually writing* the text? That's never discussed. There's no extended critique of the structure of academia.

I think this has had incredibly perverse effects. When they teach anthropology now, they make it sound like we were all a bunch of evil racist imperialists, and then maybe in the 70s or 80s we all just suddenly woke up. In fact, if you look at matters institutionally, it would be just as easy to argue exactly the opposite is the case. Back in the 1960s, there was a huge scandal, Project Camelot, when they discovered anthropologists were being used by the CIA and Pentagon in places like Chile and Vietnam. After a year or two of debate, the AAA (American Anthropological Association) banned such collaboration. After 2001 there was a similar scandal when they discovered the US military was using anthropologists as part of the occupation of Afghanistan and Iraq—a pure colonial venture in every sense of the term. And you know, it took *years* for anyone to do anything about it. This despite all the endless self-criticism about the colonial legacy of anthropology.

In effect, the discipline ended up *less* willing to act against colonialism than they had in the 60s! Why? Well, in the 60s, it was easy to get people to take moral stands because there were lots of jobs and job security. By the 00s, you have this army of marginalized, casualized adjunct professors desperately trying to hang on, being paid maybe a couple thousand a course with no benefits, so if the Army shows up and says "Hey I'll give you $100,000 a year to sell your soul. Anyway you'll save lives, because we're idiots, and if you give us commonsense advice it will almost certainly lead to us killing less innocent people!" well, *some* of them are going to take the offer. But these were exactly the issues the post-modern turn critics *didn't* address—the application of corporate management techniques and extreme forms of exploitation on campuses in the 80s, for example.

**ATZ:** That is fascinating and horrifying.

**DG:** Right? The other point people don't often make, which I think is very important is that right around the 80s when you have the critique of anthropology, the critique of colonial forms of knowledge made it very difficult to ignore the intellectual life of the rest of the world. But there was too much intellectual life going on in the rest of the world!

Let me explain what I mean by that. Say it's the 1960s or 1970s and I want to write a history of the concept of "love" or "friendship" or "religion." Well, it's still considered acceptable to stick entirely to the Western canon: to start with the Greek lyric poets or Plato and then maybe proceed through the troubadours to the Marquis de Sade to, I don't know, something by Giles Deleuze or Giorgio Agamben. Or maybe if I'm really adventurous I would start with some random Amazonian tribe and let them stand in for all non-Western humanity, *then* go to Plato.

But as time goes on, this becomes harder to justify. Can you really completely ignore the experience of every literary and philosophical tradition, China, India, Latin America? I suspect this became a crisis, because there are just so many intellectual traditions, no one can know it all. It gets to crisis when you start pointing out, well, why stick to written traditions? There are Maori or Bemba or Onandaga ideas about love or friendship that are just as sophisticated. All this stuff was terribly emotionally charged in America because on the one hand everyone is hyper-sensitive of the possibility of being accused of racism. But on the other, the prospect of everyone becoming familiar with anthropology was just too daunting. The only solution was to reject the discipline altogether, to effectively say it's not racist to ignore anthropology because anthropology itself is racist! All those texts are not forms of knowledge; they are themselves forms of imperialism.

Politically I think this was disastrous. The ultimate effect was to limit radicals to random sniping within the so-called "Western tradition," while at the same time undermining any sense of social possibility beyond it. The real radical potential of anthropology, for me at least, has always been that it compels us to see humans as much more than we have been encouraged to imagine. So I find that the attack on anthropology is in many ways reactionary politics dressed up as radicalism. It's also entirely consistent with the Puritanism that pervades so much of American intellectual life, one where politics is a frantic struggle for dominance by trying to prove one despises oneself more than anybody else. If you imagine the compendium of social possibilities that anthropology has put together over the years, not as a resource that belongs to all humankind but as a kind of guilty secret—well, my dirty little secret is still *my* dirty little secret, and it's still secret, isn't it? It's a way of keeping possession by self-abnegation.

One hundred or even fifty years ago the key anthropological theoretical terms were drawn from the people being studied: totem, taboo, mana, potlatch, and so forth. At that point, philosophers were very interested in anthropology, whether it is Freud's *Totem and Taboo* or Wittgenstein's *Remarks on Frazer* or Sartre or Bataille on the potlatch... But so were non-academic readers. In America, if garage sales are anything to go by, it seems like every family that had books at least had a copy of Linton's *Tree of Culture*, or something by Ruth Benedict or Margaret Mead lying around. Nowadays anthropologists draw all their theoretical terms from Continental philosophy and nobody cares. Why should they? If you want to know what Deleuze or Agamben think you can read the original.

**MBK:** How do you situate the question of political engagement in anthropology?

**DG:** Well I'm not sure there's only one answer to that.

Fifteen years ago I wrote in *Fragments* that anthropology has built up a compendium of human possibility, one which carries in it a certain responsibility. I still think that. Activists involved in social movements, who are interested in transforming society, tend to be fascinated with anthropology. For the most part they couldn't care less about what passes for politicized anthropology—at least, they aren't interested in "post-modern" reflections on the anthropologists' own power, which is largely just bourgeois narcissism—but they are very interested in getting a sense of alternative political, social, economic arrangements. So if nothing else I think that we should make this information available. I've also suggested we can use the tools of ethnography to tease out some of the tacit principles, the deep logic underlying certain forms of action—political action, in this case—and offer them back again, as a kind of gift. This is what anthropologists are best at, after all. For instance, to say "If one were to create an economic system based on what you seem to be doing politically, perhaps it might look like this..."

## Anthropology as art

**ATZ:** I see a link between "anthropology as a compendium of possibility" and Mehdi's idea that "contemporary art is a compendium of demonstrations of evil." There's an attempt, and quite a successful one, to frame academic discourse as science rather than as art right? But in this sense, as anthropology and art tend towards the same exposition of the possibility, we may be able to approach questions of violence and authorship from a different angle.

**ND:** Well art and anthropology are similar projects They both claim to approach the absolute particular, to understand its unique integrity, and by doing so, to speak to the universal—since both are all about defining what is ultimately human.

**DG:** That's interesting. You know Franz Boas defined anthropology as a science, but he defined it as a science of the particular, akin to geography. A geologist, or physicist, he said, is only interested in a particular river or rock because it might tell him something about rivers or rocks in general, and that about universal natural laws. A geographer actually cares about *that* river, or *that* rock, she wanted to understand a particular landscape and how it came about, and insofar as she brought in the laws of geology or physics, it was to help her do so. So once again, the general is only valuable as the servant of the particular. Anthropology, he said, was like geography; it wasn't so much interested in establishing universal laws of human nature as it's in understanding a particular culture, or ritual, or custom.

Was he right? I'm not sure. But the argument sticks in my head because there's such a resonance with what happens in consensus decision-making: that is, with the feminist ideal of a care ethic, where instead of starting out from abstract universal principles of justice, you start because you care deeply about some unique, singular human being (or relationship, or situation) and bring universality to bear in doing so. Nel Noddings even argues that caring relations are themselves a bit like art, in that they are founded on a kind of playfully creative interaction with the singularity of the person you are caring for.

**ND:** Well, aesthetics isn't just about the particular. The beauty of an equation is just as much an aesthetic phenomenon. It's obviously got to be a dialectic.

**DG:** Yes, I guess it would have to be.

**ND:** Think of all the modernists who read anthropology, archaeology, who spent years studying art from Africa, Asia, trying to find the universal principles underlying art creation. That was the very opposite of looking at each cultural tradition as a unique value in itself. But that's also because they were mostly revolutionaries who were aware that we're in a world of violent inequalities where cultures are not, presently, on the same footing. You can't just declare them all equal and make the problem go away. So they were trying to construct a universal humanity out of the shattered fragments. It's the same with how they treat individual artists nowadays. Each is treated as if he were a cultural universe unto himself—or artists are expected to be universes, and if they can't, they are failed artists. This is extraordinarily cruel.

**DG:** Sounds like we're back to the same problem we were talking about culture as text; if anthropology is art, who's the artist, and what are the political implications?

**ATZ:** Yes and no. Yes, the same questions apply, without which it wouldn't be a worthwhile parallel, but their repercussions aren't quite the same. Who the artist is and what political implications their work contains are integral parts of the way we view a work of art, as we should an anthropological text, but no one has ever thought to cancel art altogether because art is often racist or its production is exploitative. Rather than letting the "professionals" be the sole repositories of these responsibilities, the content and production of art is problematized by a much wider community. The flaws of art are taken into consideration as symptomatic of the ills of the entire social sphere, and that of course has to do with the distribution of art within that social sphere. Perhaps it should be so with anthropology as well, made available to all as a compendium of possibility.

**DG:** I couldn't agree more. German Romantics argued that everyone was an artist, effectively, until it was beaten out of them in school. Certainly in this day and age everyone is an anthropologist, since life is an endless moving back and forth between cultural universes. The question is one of which arts, which forms of anthropological insight, receive institutional recognition.

**ND:** But I think Assia is overstating the degree to which art nowadays breaks out of "professional" circles. Really the art world is a kind of miniature replica of the three principles David was just laying out as coming together in our idea of the state: violence, administration, and charisma. It's set up in such a way that it can simulate complete freedom, but carefully organized in such a way that nothing you say or do could possibly have any real democratizing effect.

We're so used to the idea that art is and necessarily has to be an elitist institution, it's hard for us to even imagine what a democratic art world would even be like. One that actually took seriously the old German Romantic ideal that we're all naturally artists, and *didn't* beat it out of us. The irony is there actually was an attempt to do this during the Russian Revolution. Everyone remembers the suppression of the Soviets. Almost no one seems aware there was a massive—and at first very successful—parallel art movement called Proletkult that involved hundreds of thousands of people. You could say the aim was to eliminate all three aspects of the state: the charismatic hero worship (cult of the artist), the top-down violence (censorship), and the bureaucracy (degrees, licensing) all at once. It was insanely popular. The organizer, Alexander Bogdanov, became the most popular political figure in the country—well, second only to Lenin. But in the end it was shut down in exactly the same way as the Soviets. Lenin removed Bogdanov and just absorbed them it the Ministry of Culture and turned it into a mere propaganda machine. Instead of workers being allowed to become artists, artists were turned into workers under bureaucratic control.

**DG:** And now no one even remembers it happened at all. I mean I had no idea until you started telling me about it.

**ND:** When it was happening, it was enormous. By the early 1920s,there were twice as many people involved in Proletkult than there were in the Communist Party. I remember reading that in Tula, which is not at all a big city, there were something like fifty different self-organized theatre groups. Communism was to be enacted immediately, as equal access to knowledge and the means not just of production but of creativity. This was the real promise of the revolution in my opinion. After all the USSR was never defeated militarily; it was defeated culturally. I'm convinced if initiatives like Proletkult hadn't been suppressed we'd have won the Cold War.

## Anthropology and economics

**DG:** In a way anthropology and economics are opposite poles in the relation of theory and practice. Economics is the discipline that has the least trouble with the idea that people will take a descriptive text and use it as a prescriptive text—sometimes it's not even clear if they make the distinction. Whereas nothing would disturb an anthropologist more than writing a book about Trobriand ritual, then coming back twenty years later to discover that Trobrianders were using it as a how-to book.

Economics sees itself a positive, predictive science, and while they're actually pretty bad at predicting anything, they have been consummate geniuses at academic politics—you'd genuinely have to go back to the Middle Ages to see any scholars that institutionally successful—with the result that, since the 80s, pretty much anybody running anything is expected to be at least familiar with economic concepts, and preferably some formal training. This even goes for charities, or left-wing magazines, anything that might seem most opposed to the spirit of Homo economicus. In order to give money away, you need to be trained in the philosophy that all people are selfish and greedy.

It's probably no coincidence that I was trained at the University of Chicago and now I'm at the London School of Economics. Both are known as the home of famous free-market ideologues (Hayek, Friedman …) and are now largely in the business of indoctrination. Each also has a world-famous anthropology department, which performs a role almost like a court jester, there to make fun of all the premises underlying economic theory. My advisor Marshall Sahlins fully embraced that role. Sahlins took the position that economics was not just ultimately theological; it emerges directly from Christian theology and shares the same basic premise of a fallen world where the human condition is one of infinite desires. Economic assumptions about scarce resources and maximizing individuals are really straight out of Augustine.

**ATZ:** Yes, "The Sadness of Sweetness."[1]

**DG:** Exactly. But Sahlins is most famous for "The Original Affluent Society."[2] In a way all his work

---

1 Marshall Sahlins, "The Sadness of Sweetness: The Native Anthropology of Western Cosmology," in *Current Anthropology*, 37(3), pp. 395–428, June 1996.
2 Marshall Sahlins, "Notes on the Original Affluent Society," in *Man the Hunter*, ed. R.B. Lee and I. DeVore (New York: Aldine Publishing Company, 1968), pp. 85–89.

continues that same basic insight that relative to what hunter-gatherers feel they need, they have plenty. They don't live in a society of scarcity because their desires are within parameters that can easily be fulfilled by their environment, with the technology they have available. In a way he's just flipping that around when he talks about theology: what is it that makes us feel that the environment is not adequate? It's really about what Mehdi calls pleonexia: the endless multiplication and expansion of desires.

Sahlins likes to point out that in much Greek philosophy, and then definitely in Christian theology, all this was premised on a fundamentally bleak view of the human condition. Why do we seek pleasure? Why are we never satisfied? Because our natural state is miserable. As Epicurus put it, pleasure is our way of forgetting about pain. But there is also an assumption that humans' essential default state is pain and suffering. Babies come into the world screaming. Because it's kind of awful here. So we seek pleasure, but it's always ultimately a temporary respite. It's a remarkably depressing view of the world.

## Freedom 1—which finite resources?

**MBK:** In the discussion of feminism we talked about incommensurability. This question of incommensurability is the same problem as the problem of capitalism: unlimited appropriation. We all know—

except Donald Trump, Nicolas Sarkozy, and Alain Badiou—we all know that the possibilities of the planet are finite. So the question of private property is no longer only a question of justice, but a question of survival. The fact, like Occupy Wall Street said, that 1% of people possess 99% of the earth resources, is not only a question of distributive justice, but now as a simple question of living, of breathing.

**ATZ:** And again, we can take that and look at it differently considering that these finite resources are only finite because of our way of selecting "resources", the decisions we have made as to what will fuel our system. I think that is to the image of a lot of things.

**ND:** Yes, because care is a limitless resource. Or philosophy.

**ATZ:** Yes, or knowledge! The more you "spend" it by sharing it the more of it there is!

**DG:** The same is true for freedom as well if you define it right.

**ATZ:** Exactly. So we are finding ourselves in this crisis because of the way we've framed our reality is dependent on resources, which are the finite ones.

**DG:** Two thoughts ahead here. The first is exactly that. What I'd really like would be to get rid of the terms production and consumption as a basis for political economy entirely, and substitute care and freedom. As feminist economists like Nancy Folbre often point out, any economic action can be seen as a form of caring labor. After all, you only build a bridge because you care that people can get across the river. You only drill for oil because you care that people can get around in cars. But there are subtleties here. Everyone would agree hospitals provide care. But what about prisons? Prison feed and clothe prisoners after all, provide them with at least some minimal level of medical care. But it seems just intuitively wrong to treat prisons as caring institutions.

Why? This is why I felt the element of freedom was essential. It's not care insofar as it imprisons you. (In fact, the more I examine the historical origins of relations of domination and the state, the more I come to believe that these things came about through the perversion of caring relations.) But in terms of definitions this allows a rather Spinozist formulation—not exactly Spinozist, but in that spirit—where "care" is any action meant to maintain or increase another person's freedom.

**ATZ:** And freedom as?

**DG:** I conceive freedom primarily in terms of play, or maybe better to say I conceive play is the highest expression of freedom, since it's self-directed activity that isn't aimed towards anything outside it, but is a value to itself.

**ND:** It's part of a game that you have to obligate everyone to accept in the moment, but tomorrow it could be another play.

**DG:** Yes, exactly, you're free to put it on or off.

**MBK:** Very interesting! I didn't know that. And that's what I'm looking for through the "utopia" of the game. In your books there are all kinds of descriptions of how societies solve their problems through ritual games. For me, the philosophical, artistic, political idea of the game, in its universal scope, is that in every game the rules are the same for everyone. We always say "all are equal before the law," but we know that's not true. The social game under the law of the market is fixed. Only when we're all effectively equal before the law, the rules—as in all effective games—freedom will be possible. This is what Adorno meant by this enigmatic sentence: "As long as the universal and the particular diverge, there is no freedom."

**DG:** Yes, that's why I speak of the "utopia of rules."

What I find fascinating about play—say children's play—is that it always generates rules. If you're just engaged in purely free, unconstrained behavior, well, it gets boring fast. Imagine you want to speak in a mock language that's entirely random, just any sound at all in no sort of order. Most of us have tried this as children. It's actually quite difficult to keep it random for any length of time. Usually what really happens is you start making up some sort of nonsense language with its own phonemic code, rhythms, patterns. To try to avoid doing so soon becomes exhausting. Sure pure play generates rules. But then rules threaten to stifle it. This is a constant tension. So freedom, for me, is precisely this, the constant play of the play principle against the rules it has created.

This is why some early twentieth-century poets felt free verse wasn't really free: "You can play tennis without a net, but it's not much of a game, is it?"—that was Robert Frost. But of course most poets would now reply that a good poem generates its own rules, its own prosody, and then of course strains against them. It's as if the poet has to create a legal universe each time, so as to be able to carry out petty or not-so-petty crimes against it.

So let's return for a moment to the opposition of care and freedom. When you thinking of a care-giving relationship, usually the first thing you think of is the relation between mother and child. Mothers take care of children so they'll grow and thrive, obviously, but in a more immediate sense, they take care of children so they can play. That's what children actually do most of the time. And play is the ultimate expression of freedom for its own sake. So why not make that the paradigm for an economy too, which is after all just the means whereby human beings provide for one another. Not least because care and freedom are infinitely expandable without destroying the planet, while production and consumption are not.

## Freedom 2—property and Kant's chiasmic structure of freedom

**DG:** You were starting to ask whether I conceived of freedom as purely derived from the inversion of slavery. The particular legal definition from the tradition that comes from Roman law really has to do with property. Property is a right which is your absolute freedom to do anything you want with your things, except those things prevented by law or force.

**MBK:** Yes but that's not true.

**DG:** Exactly. It's not true at all. Even insofar as you can make it true, it's an idiotic way to define a property relationship. Okay, so here I have a gun—or even just a car. I can do anything I want with my car except what is forbidden by law and force. What does that even mean? That I'm free to attach sequins to it or break it up for scrap metal? Pretty much anything else I can do with my car, how and where I can drive it, park it, is strictly regulated. The only *absolute* right I have is my right to stop anyone *else* from using it. You can only imagine property rights as a relationship between a person and an object because in effect it's a right you have "against all the world" concerning the disposition of that object. A relation between you and everyone in the entire world is hard to get your head around; one with an object is not. But in another sense you can't have a "relation" with an object; that's just as absurd. As medieval jurists quickly pointed out when they revived Roman law in the twelfth century: if you're on a desert island, you might have a deeply personal relationship with a tree; who knows you might have long talks with it every day, in fact, but it's not a *property* relation. If there are two people on the island, however, then you might have to work out some arrangement about who gets to sit under the tree.

**MBK:** With Kant freedom is defined as the way you interiorize the law. So it was the first time perhaps in the history of thought that freedom becomes subjective and becomes the point of view of the slave. That's what's very interesting with Kant. Usually freedom is the point of view of the master or the point of view of the bourgeois.

**DG:** You need to tell me more about this. I have to be honest and say Kant's conception of freedom never made a lot of sense to me. Yes, in order to have morality you have to say people have free will. Fair enough, but in order to justify saying human action is not determined, and therefore free, Kant feels he has to attribute it to a noumenal self outside of time which is autonomous in the sense of making its own law. Okay. Both existing outside time and the freedom to create law were statuses previously attributed only to God (well, the second maybe a little also to kings, but only insofar as kings were, effectively, gods), so at this point you almost feel you're in the presence of something genuinely radical. But the moment you do, he brings in universal rationality—which of course in medieval theology would have been yet another aspect of God—which dictates that unless you are slave to your passions, that is, if you exercise genuine freedom, you always freely choose to do the rational thing, which he says is to act morally. So you are the absolute sovereign who then discovers he's really just the slave.

Does something like this have to happen if you try to create a world based on such extreme radical individualism, that the promises or commitments we make to each other, or even just our interactions with each other, aren't seen as in any sense producing us, making us what we are, but are always some kind of secondary phenomenon, since the only really important moral relation we have isn't to anyone else (our neighbors, for that matter, our mothers ...) but to some kind of total abstraction, God, Reason, the Law, the Cosmos, whatever it may be? Some kind of hypostasized absolute? I guess it must be. But I still can't understand how a being outside time *does* anything!

**MBK:** You think against Kant, I think *with* Kant against Kant. One must think Kant in spite of himself, despite his aporia or his excesses. I maintain that what Kant achieved was the discovery of a paradoxical identity between freedom and constraint. The inner noumenal freedom. Hegel will see very well that it is the *interiorized* freedom, that is to say the relation of master to slave.

**DG:** Agreed, I think that was more or less what I was trying to get at too when I talked about property. Our conceptions of freedom are derived from Roman law, ultimately, I'd say, from Roman slave law. We can imagine property as a relation of person and thing, despite the obvious absurdities, because it traces back to a legal relation in which the thing actually *is* a person, just a person who by force and law is rendered a thing, a "speaking implement," as the Romans put it. Freedom is just the arbitrary will of the master. So far so good.

**MBK:** Yes, the freedom of constraint that Kant attributes to pure noumenal spontaneity outside of time goes back to the existence, in the only anthropo-logical enclosure, of the master-servitude relation. The example that I always give to illustrate this fact is the simple fact of getting dressed: if I decide not to dress to go out, I certainly have a "free" act, but that will lead me either to prison or to the asylum. A fine example of a purely internalized law, or it's an abstract Other who connects me to dress me, and therefore has a very concrete effect on me. My "spontaneous" freedom, as a human noumenon, is absolute constraint.

**DG:** Yes that's also a nice way to frame the paradox of possessive individualism, as with the car which is the symbol of absolute freedom, where in fact every aspect of what you can do behind the wheel is meticulously regulated. But it does help me clar-ify something: that the noumenal self is just a fan-tasy created by legal relations of domination. But if we speak of "freedom" this way, how is it different from what an economist or "rational choice theo-rist" would say, which is that everyone is free. The slave is free too, because he has the choice of obey-ing orders or being whipped to death?

**MBK:** Because for Kant—and this is what's really powerful in Kant—human freedom (what I call ple-onasm) is *born* of constraint. This is because we are forced to bend to rules other than those of mere ani-mal survival, such as getting dressed, cleaning up, working, etc. In short, it's because we voluntarily put ourselves in prison (and observe how there's no example of the phenomenon of imprisonment in any species other than our own) that we then become susceptible to positive freedom, such as creating art works, livable political regimes, scientific discoveries, etc.

**DG:** So you're saying a sacrifice of negative freedom is the necessary condition for any meaningful exercise of positive freedom?

**MBK:** There's a real and painful paradox there, but it can't just be brushed away. It's because we humans are animals of gratuitous constraint that we're also animals of positive freedom. And indeed the idea of God in Kant would be that of a pure noumenon who would finally be free from all constraint, which is a brilliant way to summarize all theology: here below, the chains; up there, pure freedom.

**DG:** Well, I know that in theological terms the great chain of being was defined in terms of rationality, with God being absolute reason, and the next highest beings, the thrones, powers, denominations, angelic beings, merely extensions of His will. So you're saying Kant democratizes the cosmos, as it were? But ultimately then he takes it back, doesn't he, by saying that rationality is universal and external and timeless?

**MBK:** There's a chiasmatic structure: the positive phenomenon of the law in the human is the negative constraint; the negative noumenon is positive freedom. It's is to Kant that we owe the discovery of this structure. Even if my reading of Kant has nothing to do with the Kantian letter, and even if I agree with your initial objections—which are of the same type as Adorno's—Kantian liberty as a freedom to submit is a hypostasis of petit-bourgeois submission, which is true. Still, among these petit-bourgeois you will also have artists, revolutionaries, scientific geniuses, that's to say people who will transform the prison that is all of human existence into the possibility of creating incredible things, which would not have been possible under any regime of pure animality whatsoever.

**DG:** That's a very beautiful formulation.

You know I'm not exactly channeling Adorno—at least I don't think I am. To be honest, I'm still thinking about that anonymous Roman magistrate. It's funny: when we speak of the classical origins of our civilization (and I'm referring at this point to a world civilization, which everyone now participates in to some degree or another), the figures that naturally come to mind are men like Pericles or Euripides or Plato, but never that guy—he doesn't even have a name—even though one could well say that he's shaped our lives in much deeper ways. The man I'm imagining is a senatorial official of the late republic or early empire, who sponsors games, renders prudent judgment on questions of property law, and then goes home to have his most intimate needs attended to by slaves who are in legal terms conquered people with no rights, and with whom he can and does do whatever he likes—rape, torture, kill, with total impunity. He's a monster. Yet his perspective on the world, his judgments, lie at the basis of all our liberal ideas about freedom, and I suspect a lot more besides.

The situation creates a series of conceptual traps. I see Kant as struggling with them as well, hence the antinomies. I think you're right that in doing so he came on a deeply human truth: that any meaningful freedom is born of submission to (but I would add, simultaneous rebellion against) arbitrary rules of our own creation. What I worry is that the brilliance of his discovery might unwittingly seduce us into accepting that peculiarly Roman view of the human condition, where instead of being dialogic creatures who create ourselves through some sort of deliberative process, we are assumed to be absolute individuals whose freedom is rooted in some sort of atrocity, who imagine ourselves not as brought into being by our relations with each other, but by our relations with some abstract totality (law, reason ...).

The question though is can you have both at the same time? Can we see the free subject as something created by its relations with others, by non-atrocious ones, and also at the same time as the creator of the constraints that are as you (and Kant) would have it, the very possibility of its freedom? It's a real puzzle. And it might sound abstract (well, okay, it is pretty abstract if you put it that way), but it has real practical implications.

## Freedom 3—friendship, play
## and quantification

**DG:** In Germanic languages, including English, the word "free" derives from "friend," because the idea is that a slave can't have friends.

**MBK:** It's interesting since we also say that rich men don't have friends.

**DG:** Or kings. When I was studying divine kingship, one common theme is that there is a hidden affinity, even kinship, between kings and slaves, because they are the only kinds of people who have no social relations other than relations of domination.

I guess I'm struggling with two ideas of freedom. On the one hand we have the idea inspired by the notion of the "ability to have friends." If you assume that people *are* the sum of relations they have or have had with others, this is self-determination. On the other, if you have the purely individualistic definition of freedom, well perhaps its inevitable you end up getting boxed in with these Roman-law property definitions I was just talking about.

**MBK:** It's a real question, because you can say that there's a far-right anarchism that is libertarian.

**DG:** Yes exactly, that right-wing version is the logical extension of that same silly dualism that produces the possessive individual: the idea that "you" are a spirit that owns your body and possessions, and therefore the freedom to do whatever you like with your arms, legs, cows, slaves, etc. Your relations with property, are somehow prior to relations with anyone else.

The alternative is to say that a free person is one who has the ability to make friends, to make commitments to others—which, from a purely liberal sense, are restraints on your freedom. This would take us back to Kant, or anyway, to Mehdi's chiasmatic structure in Kant, but perhaps (I hope) with the shadow of the Roman magistrate now finally in retreat. This non-liberal notion of freedom is defined by your ability to voluntarily enter into relations of constraint and get out of them again. Freedom is the ability to make promises, which is precisely what slaves *can't* do.

The question is how to square that conception with the sense of freedom as play—as autopoiesis, if you like, the self-generation or self-organization of systems (though that might not be the best term to use, since it's been taken up in very specific ways by biology and systems theory.)

My own way of framing it has been through the opposition of play and games. Now, in English this is especially easy to express because there are distinct words for play and games, a distinction which for some odd reason doesn't seem to exist in any other human language—at least, none I'm aware of.

**MBK:** And what is the distinction?

**ATZ:** Play is immanent; it's something you do and its purpose is itself. Children in a sandbox play. Games have a design, a delineated space and time, rules, stakes—and somebody wins.

**DG:** Precisely. You can "play" a game—which means following an explicit set of rules—or you can just play around, which is pure improvisation. So when I was describing freedom as the tension between play and the rules it generates, another way to say that would be the relationship between play and games. On the one hand, pure self-directed activity for its own sake is also the exercise of freedom for its own sake, as a form of pleasure in itself. But just as (as I was saying earlier) if you try to speak pure nonsense, you quickly start creating something that sounds like a language, exercising freedom for its own sake will inevitably generate rules. Why? I think it's partly because we play for pleasure, and being entirely random isn't a lot of fun. If you try to make noises in an entirely random fashion that sounds nothing like a language, it might be enjoyable for a very short period of time, but if you keep it up for more than a minute or two, it quickly starts to feel like work. What's fun is setting up a pattern and playing around with it. So play generates games. Freedom by this logic—at least it seems to me that this is the best way to think of it—is the tension between the play and the rules it generates. But that tension is also one of our major forms of pleasure.

So this might be one way to synthesize the two conceptions of freedom. Play also turns into games the moment there is more than one person playing. What's more, both freedom as the capacity to create games and freedom as the capacity to make promises are expressions of pure creativity, but ones which create something to which one is bound—but not absolutely.

**ATZ:** Unless they are quantified, in which case it becomes absolute and that is the issue! So the other difference between play and game is that in one nobody keeps count, or does so without record. When we "play for nothing" we don't keep track of scores, whereas in games you do. It is quantification and record-keeping that corrupts the relation between play and game. Our ability to move between them is corrupted when the winners of a game suddenly refuse to start from scratch again once the game is over. Which I guess is why people like the Nuer or Dinka didn't understand why having lost a war with the British meant prolonged subservience. As far as they could tell, they'd just lost a game. Similarly, our ability to make promises is corrupted when we lose the ability to break them, which happens when the promise is quantified and recorded as a debt.

And so it's our ability to actively consent to rules but also our ability to renegotiate them which is corrupted under the reign of supreme quantification, where mathematics is considered the only transcendental truth. So if the winners are always the same, and all promises are to be kept no matter the consequences, you end up in a class society based on a debt economy.

**DG:** Oh very nice! Yes it's not a promise if you can't break it: this was one of my great realizations when I was writing *Debt*.

You realize though, by this particular gambit, Assia, you're effectively doing the same thing: challenging me to make my own rather playful formulation into something at least potentially more enduring.

Ok. I'll give it a shot.

Well, first of all I guess you could say there are two levels here (maybe three?). Quantifying, by turning play into game, introduces the possibility of enduring effects. But just the possibility. We can play poker for chips and wipe the slate clean every evening. But we can also insist on cashing the chips in for real money—or the chips themselves can become money, which apparently did sometimes happen in some towns in Southeast Asia, where you could use mahjong chips to buy things in the marketplace.

Ritual—according to many anthropological versions of ritual theory, anyway—is about the annihilation of history. It means subsuming historical events (a marriage, a death, the dedication of a monument, the granting of a license to practice medicine, conquest...) that might seem to make a permanent difference, into a larger cosmic order where they don't really matter, because nothing can ever change. That's why Levi-Strauss claimed that when games do appear in ritual, they always end in a tie. (I don't think that's really true by the way.) But there are some games that threaten to break out of that ritual framework. War is like that. Elaine Scarry once asked a very interesting question about war. She said it's easy to see why enemies might wish to resolve their differences through some sort of contest. But why does it have to be a contest of injuring? Why not just shame and humiliate each other in some sort of way? Why do they have to physically hurt each other?

The traditional answer is Clausewitz's: that a contest of violence carries in it the means of its own enforcement, the loser can't just declare they don't accept the outcome and stomp off, because then the winner can just shoot him. But that explanation doesn't really work for a whole series of reasons. Scarry proposes we think instead of the very permanence of what war does to human bodies: death and disfigurement, maiming, scars... Violence doesn't create the means of its own enforcement so much as it creates the means of its own memorialization. It carves monuments in ruined flesh you are unable to forget. Or in our terms here, you can't simply reshuffle the cards and start again. You're almost obliged to come up with a reason why all those permanent injuries had some kind of permanent meaning.

This is why it might seem, on the surface, why in the early Middle Ages, for instance, you have so many law codes that mainly consist of specifying what monetary compensation is due not just for people killed in feuds, wars, and the like, but also often very detailed schedules of injury: this much for each severed finger, this much for an eye that's been destroyed, etc. It occurs to me, now that I think about it, that these are all *permanent* injuries. Nobody seeks compensation for a broken leg, even if—as a modern lawyer would undoubtedly point out—it renders the victim unable to work or do much of anything for a considerable period of time. You pay for injuries that never go away. Despite the fact that money—whatever they're using as money, whether it's cows, or silver, or marten pelts—is by definition the form of wealth that's most ephemeral, that wipes away history with each transaction. It's an attempt to deny history. To pretend things can be reshuffled that everyone knows really can't be. It's almost as if you are acknowledging the permanence of the wound by the very inadequacy of the compensation. You can't really shove it back into ritual again, but everyone agrees to pretend you can.

## Freedom 4—critical realism, emergent levels of freedom

**MBK:** I once wrote that the role of language is to change things by missing them. Words always miss the thing. Language is always a simplification of things, but a powerful one. It's a simplification that creates a complexification beyond language. It's a constant race between language and the way we have influence on it.

**DG:** When you say that ontology doesn't explain freedom or that when it does it just turns it into pure contingency... Well I guess that depends on your ontology! My own background to this in the Anglophone world is in Roy Bhaskar's critical realism, which claims to embed freedom in the deep structure of reality itself.

Basically, Bhaskar states that emergent levels of reality are levels of increasing freedom. Bhaskar is a transcendental realist, and mostly known (insofar as he's known at all) as a philosopher of science, though in fact his interest in scientific questions is ultimately entirely political. So he asks: why are scientific experiments possible, but at the same time why are scientific experiments necessary? Typically philosophers of science focus on one or the other, not both. On the one hand, why is it possible to create situations where you can predict exactly what will happen each time you do it? On the other, why is it so difficult? Why does it take so much work? Why is it impossible to predict anything in real-life "open systems" like, say, the weather? His answer is, as he calls it, a "depth ontology," the very opposite of a flat ontology. This is where emergence comes in.

Bhaskar talks about emergence in the same way you talk about "events." The aspect of reality described by biology is emergent from the level described by physics, animals from plants, and so on. At each level of complexity you could also, he says, speak about a greater degree of freedom. Freedom does exist on a subatomic level, but pretty minimally: a tree is more free than an electron or electro-magnetic field; a bird is more free than a tree, and so forth.

**ATZ:** Well, I don't know so much about quantum physics, but shouldn't it be that on a subatomic level there is a lot?

**DG:** That's where I got ludic pan-psychism.

**MBK:** I'm scandalized!

**DG:** [*laughs*] I was intending to avoid that whole issue. Okay, well, there's a lively debate about this among physicists, as I understand it. Physicists can themselves be pretty playful. They're not at all like biologists, who tend to be incredibly doctrinaire—but then, I guess unlike biologists, physicists don't have to worry about crazy religious fanatics trying to disprove their basic assumptions, so that allows them to relax a bit more, to have a bit more fun. So physicists do in fact debate whether the fact that you can't predict the direction electrons will jump should be taken to mean they have some minimal form of intentionality!

**MBK:** I'm on the side of those who believe that it's our measuring instruments that create the intention.

**ATZ:** Sure, but as per our earlier points it could be true, because by attempting to measure it we allow the electron to have freedom (intentionality) because we give them a rule to play with? The electrons are asked by us to make a choice, like in that simple experiment of electrons shooting through a piece of paper, and so they do.

**MBK:** A very interesting point of view.

**DG:** It is.

What occurred to me is that if an electron had intentionality, in however embryonic a sense—or, if you like, if it can be said to have something which on a more complex emergent level becomes "intentionality", if there is directedness that can be attributed to it... well, what sort of directedness would that be? Because you can't possibly apply a utilitarian perspective to an electron. For an economist—or a rational-choice theorist, all intentional action aims to maximize some interest, usually self-interest. Electrons have no self interest. It's impossible to imagine them acting out of selfish motives (or altruistic ones, for that matter.)

Or I guess nothing is impossible, but it would be awfully silly and I've never seen anyone actually try.

This is why the whole phenomenon of animal play—an issue I was put on to by my old friend Erica Lagalisse, that all animals play, and the fact that they do upsets our normal assumptions about the universe—is such a problem for animal behaviorists. Birds, fish, even lobsters and insects, seem to engage in at least some behavior that might be considered the exercise of their most complex capacities just for the sake of exercising them. Even Kropotkin, when he wrote about mutual aid, Erica pointed out, described flocks of birds that would perform complex coordinated maneuvers just because they could. Animal cooperation wasn't just pragmatic; often, animals cooperated just for fun. But why should this surprise us? We assume that beings have a desire for self preservation, that life, as Nietzsche I think said, "desires itself." But if life is a capacity for action, then why shouldn't the exercise of those fullest capacities for their own sake be a logical extension of that same principle? You don't want to preserve yourself to just sit there, because then you're not actually preserving yourself, you might as well be dead.

Biologists have a real problem with this. Of course most have no problem at all talking about "selfish genes"; in fact strands of DNA are almost the only thing other than humans (or at best certain vertebrates) that scientists feel entirely comfortable attributing intentions too—even though they will often disavow what they're doing by making some transparent alibi, saying "Of course this is all just a metaphor" before proceeding entirely as if it were literally true—because for them, being "scientific" means only attributing rational motives to intentional actors, and "rational" motives are apparently selfish ones. If you can't ascribe selfish motives, you just don't say anything at all.

So it occurred to me: let's imagine an electron was acting with some kind of embryonic intentionality. What would that electron—or self-organizing electro-magnetic field or crystalline structure or what-have-you—be doing then? It can only be a desire to experience freedom for its own sake!

**ATZ:** Yeah exactly. The universe playing so that God can have a hug.

**DG:** Exactly, its play.

**MBK:** There are two points of view, and I'll try to make a dialectic link between them. First, do you place freedom in the principle of entanglement?

**DG:** I don't know. Do I?

**MBK:** Because it can be interpreted as the opposite, like ultra-cosmic Spinozist codetermination, where freedom has no place.

**DG:** True. It can be. And, I'd definitely agree, freedom could never be the *only* principle. Wasn't it Charles Sanders Peirce who developed Nietzsche's idea that it would be possible to generate all physical laws from a single principle that if something happens it's more likely to happen again? You could easily balance a principle of play against a principle of *that*.

**ATZ:** "That" being a tendency to recur?

**DG:** Yes. The problem with Peirce's principle standing alone is that if you assume anything that happens, any random conjuncture, is more likely to happen again... well, you can start with an entirely random cosmos and eventually end up with what looks like what we have now, a cosmos governed by what look to us like laws. But there's no reason it should stop; eventually, everything should become entirely fixed. The universe would become more organized over time, which, at least if you believe in the Big Bang, does seem to be the case. But it would eventually become absolutely uniform and predictable. You'd end up with that Spinozist cosmos, or Pythagorean music of the spheres. But that doesn't seem to be what is happening.

**ATZ:** But then again, most things have opposing forces. You're essentially describing chaos and order. Maybe it's entropy...

**DG:** This might sound silly, but I've always been a little suspicious of the second law of thermodynamics. I'm not denying that the principle of entropy applies within a closed system. Obviously it does. But it certainly doesn't apply to any of the systems we care about the most. Neither the earth, since we have the sun feeding us energy continually, nor the universe as a whole, which has obviously become more complex and organized since the Big Bang. Okay, so self-contained chemical systems tend to become disorganized over time. So? What are we to make of a law where everything important that happens is an exception?

**ATZ:** We should really invite a physicist…

**DG:** I've always felt the law of entropy was invented by depressed Victorians anticipating the inevitable decline of their empire. It's the sigh of the not-particularly-oppressed creature, indignant that his power won't last forever, since nothing does. You put your bird in a cage, then complain it's going to die. Get over it!

But to get back to Bhaskar, since I didn't quite finish my summary. What he's saying is that you have these different emerging levels of complexity, and not only does each one have a greater degree of freedom (or arbitrariness, from the perspective of determination) but how they interact in an open system is inherently unpredictable, because you have causative mechanisms from different emergent levels interacting. That's why you need to have a scientific experiment, therefore eliminating mechanisms from all but one emergent level, to understand how any one mechanism works. Closed systems are always human creations and they typically require an enormous amount of work.

## Freedom 5—negotiating the rules
## of the game

**DG:** The point I made in *The Utopia of Rules* which is related to this is that the other pleasure of games is not just that you voluntarily submit to the rules, but also that you know exactly what they are. In everyday life you're constantly playing games whose rules ... well, sometimes they're a total mystery, but more often you kind of have a sense of what they are, but you're never quite sure. And yes, some people who are consummate performers, they have a real sense of artistry about these things. And they don't need to know the rules; they just have an intuitive sense of what a right move is. But most of us are stumbling around like bad amateur sociologists trying to figure it all out. In a proper game, you know exactly who the players are, what the rules are, how you know when you won ... In real life all of that is at least a little up for grabs and it's annoying.

**ATZ:** Which is maybe why we all become so attached to enforcing the rules of games when we do know them. So excitedly you hear yourself screaming "Oh you can't do that!" during card games

**DG:** Yes, or those people who when they really want to insult someone say "He cheats at solitaire!" Well, why the hell shouldn't you cheat at solitaire if you feel like it? Who are you cheating? God?

But when you're dealing with other people, there's the even more difficult fact that there's always at least two levels of a real-life game: the level governed by rules, and the level where you're negotiating what exactly those rules are to begin with. It's considered impolite to talk about this. Actually I've noticed that's one of the most disturbing things about talking to schizophrenics: often they *do* talk about it; they have a tendency to spell everything out. So if you try to move in a direction which will confront them with some logical inconsistency or delusional premise, they'll just immediately try to lay down new rules: "No we're not talking about that! We're talking about this!"

Among polite people, rules are established indirectly. This is even true when the rules allow a great deal of physical violence. I spent a lot of time trying to figure out exactly how the process worked while I was involved in direct action campaigns in America in 2000, 2001. Street actions often took the form of something very much like urban warfare, with each side, activists and cops, trying to scout the other side's deployments, overwhelm their positions, outflank or outmanoeuver one another, and so forth. Always, in direct action, there are tacit rules of engagement: what kind of weapons and tactics can be used by each side. Activists can't engage in overt violence; police can't actually do anything likely to kill anyone, etc. Occasionally—very occasionally—the rules could be worked out directly, by negotiation. This used to be true in Italy in the days of the Tute Bianche, most of whose leadership, I'mgiven to understand, had contacts with people on the other side, mostly kids they'd known in grade school who had the misfortune of becoming policemen. So the Tute Bianche would put on these giant goofy padded outfits—so they were essentially like cartoon characters, lumbering, ungainly, but indestructible—and they'd call the cops and say "Okay so you can hit us as hard as you like, as long as you just hit us on the padding. We won't hit you. We'll just try to crash through the barricades. Let's see who wins!" And the cops played along. For the most part. Some of my Italian friends told me that despite the fact the activists were famous for wrapping themselves in inflatable inner tubes, for the first couple years, none of the police even brought a pin. But then came the G8 in Genoa, and a fascist, Fini, was put in charge of the police operation, and the activists knew something terrible was about to happen because suddenly the cops wouldn't pick up the phone.

All that was extremely unusual though. Usually negotiation is carried out indirectly, perhaps to a degree through legal and parliamentary means, but mainly through the media. So there was a level of symbolic, even mythological warfare on top of the actual warfare. The anarchists would create silly-looking giant puppets and appear with tubas and belly dancers to make the police response seem crazed and disproportionate. The cops would respond by trying to convince the public that the puppets might really contain bombs or hydrochloric acid to throw in their faces. The anarchists would build a giant catapult to launch stuffed animals at the summit castle. The press would pretend the stuffed animals had really been doused in gasoline and set on fire. And the success of these symbolic campaigns was crucial in determining just how much force each side thought that they could get away with. Each side then accused the other—though they couldn't quite put it this way—of cheating, of refusing to play by the rules.

**ND:** Most revolutions happen not because people are starving but because somebody is breaking the rules to a degree that people won't stand for it anymore.

**DG:** Well, if people are literally starving, they're usually not really in a position to revolt. But it's true. You can't get really mad at someone unless you live in the same moral universe. This is something I noticed when I was in Madagascar. I only knew that I was truly socially accepted when people started getting angry at me. During the first six months I was in Arivonimamo, and if I did something and someone felt what I did was entirely out of line, they wouldn't get mad at me, but at whatever Malagasy person they thought should have taught me better. If they got mad at *me*, that meant they saw me as a full moral person.

It struck me that most likely, most people who ever lived, who lived under governments, didn't see their rulers as moral persons in that sense. Certainly that was true in Madagascar. Most rural people there think of the government in the same way we think of a hurricane: the government might blow through and threaten to reek havoc with your life; you try to get out of the way, you deal with the consequences ... It has force-of-nature status. But it would never occur to you to say "Those gendarmes really shouldn't have been collaborating with the bandits like that," or "The French governor general was wrong to raise taxes." Poor people (and I come from a poor family and spent most of my life poor) see landlords in the same way. Actually I still remember my first year in grad school in Chicago. I had a rich friend in the same program, and we were both renting apartments in the same building, and he kept getting indignant when the landlord didn't fulfill some contractual obligation. It really puzzled me. He's a landlord! What do you expect? You don't get angry at a landlord. They operate by an alien logic, inimical to our own. And maybe you try to play them, but if you're smart, you try to stay under their radar like you would any figure of authority, because if they notice you at all, it'll probably mean trouble.

In fact I think it was that observation which led me to conclude that middle classness isn't an economic category but a moral one. If you see a cop and feel more safe, not less, you're probably middle class. Middle-class people are people who feel the institutional structure (the schools, the banks, the government…) should be there to *serve* them, and get indignant if it they don't.

Well, in that sense most people in the Third World don't feel especially middle class. But when enough of them begin to feel the government are at least moral persons, whose actions *could* be judged by criterium of right and wrong, that's when rebellions happen.

In Madagascar in the 1940s there was an emerging middle class. Enough people were educated and drawn into the world of the French civil service and larger colonial universe that they saw French people as moral beings who they could judge by right or wrong. The result was the revolt of 1947.

My friend Lauren Leve found something very similar in Nepal. She had been doing a project on a rural women's literacy and empowerment campaign done by an international NGO, trying to expose all the liberal assumptions underlying the program—that it was really preparing people for microcredit and bourgeois aspirations. A few years later she came back and half the women who'd been through the program were Maoist guerillas.

So that's a real danger. If you draw people into your game, they might decide you're cheating.

**ND:** It's very interesting that in Russian friend is [*drook*], which means the Other. So the friend is the other that you negotiate with always.

**MBK:** It is a central question in love affairs: do we play the same game or is it different?

**DG:** Well love as a game is the very definition of a situation in which the rules aren't clear.

**MBK:** Sometimes they are. In my work I'm interested in BDSM because of this.

**DG:** Oh true. In that case the rules may even be specified in writing.

**ND:** So fair games are only ones where all rules are clear.

**MBK:** Life is a series of unclear games, so in that it's fascist.

**DG:** That's the thing about love though … Let's talk two poles of this. A BDSM couple, that's the extreme of total clarity, whereas romantic love is the exact opposite. There are so many things you can and can't do and can and can't say but it's entirely unclear. And if you tried to map out the rules, you'd be breaking the most important one!

**MBK:** So I would say that romantic love at its pinnacle is the moment when you're playing a perfect game of unformulated rules. That's what's magical about it, but it often doesn't work long-term.

**DG:** It's happy fascism, then? But yes, often it needs to be rationalized eventually.

**ND:** [*laughs mischievously*]

**ATZ:** I feel that!

**MBK:** And to be an anarchist is to be creating the rules with the others at every moment, not just being against the system of rules.

**DG:** Yeah otherwise you're just rebellious.

**MBK:** I would say that politics in the generic sense of term is a game that's is looking for its own rules, and that's why anarchism is perhaps the essence of politics.

# Play fascism

**MBK:** Reality begins in fascism, to put it very violently. In the psychological sense of the term it's very difficult for me to accept that, but philosophically I force myself to accept it so as to be less scandalized and act more.

**DG:** I'm not quite sure which "reality" We're referring to here, but I think I can add something. This is why I suggested that you look at the book on kings. The evidence seems to be that it's perhaps the case that the origin of order is in fascism, but what might be called play fascism! So we do get to the idea of play here. There are things that look like royal burials that go back thirty thousand years, with enormous amounts of goods that other people weren't buried with: scepters, beautiful garments of various kinds … and these were mammoth hunters. But almost every single one of them were physically deformed in some way, so either they were dwarfs or giants or hunchbacks.

There is a kin of giddy theatricality here. Almost as if power begins as burlesque, as a parody of a real power that has hitherto only been imagined.

**MBK:** Yeah but it's like in reality—superheroes or blockbusters with big robots. When Hollywood produces such films it's a metaphor of power. I learned this reading your work. When Hollywood represents monsters as coming from the outside, it's a self-portrait. They are the monstrous robots, the gigantic machines, etc. I read it as deformity in the anthropological closure. The dimension of anthropology in my work is very anti-Nietzschean; it's what he calls the degenerated, the losers, the weak, etc. They are the ones I do philosophy for. With diaphanes we want to do a review on madness, asking real mad people the question of social inadequacy and of the political content of their incurable madness.

**DG:** Perhaps power begins with a celebration of madness. Certainly there's an ongoing link between prophets, freakishness, sovereignty, and madness which never goes away. If you look at it anthropologically, it makes sense that the very first political figures are also strangely deformed. There is apparently no part of the world (Persia, China, Peru ...) where royal courts didn't host dwarfs. "The state" begins as a kin of the circus, and always to some degree remains so.

One of the articles that I thought was most revealing about this was an article about Nuer prophets by Tom Beidelman. The Nuer are a famously egalitarian people with a segmentary lineage structure whereby everyone is descended from a single ancestor and knows exactly how they are related to everyone else. Different clans and lineages are constantly feuding with one another, but it's always mediated by this very complex kinship system and legal system, even though there are no political authorities at all. They have these madmen that are normally kind of like the village idiot, but when there's a crisis, or things that require large organization, they find one of them to become a charismatic leader. So every Nuer village is surrounded by these people who are sort of arranging shells and talking to themselves in languages that no one can understand and hanging upside down from the rafters, and as you might imagine they often have physical deformities and are given to unconventional sexual habits…

**MBK:** I don't imagine, I identify [*laughs*].

**DG:** They're probably who we'd be if we happened to have been turn-of-the-century Nuer. Normally everyone just laughs at them, but when something terrible happens—there's an epidemic, a war between groups and they have to figure out a way to resolve it, somebody invades, things which are through their very universality evidence of the violent intrusion of divinity in its most universal aspect—then suddenly one of them will pop up and become leader. They're like a reserve of talent. Social movements form around them.

Pierre Clastres made the argument that stateless societies such as the Nuer, or those anthropologists have studied in Amazonia, Melanesia, and so forth, are stateless by choice. Insofar as they exist, political offices such as chief tend to be hedged about by elaborate safeguards. Basically they're made so onerous and difficult for anyone who holds them that they can't possibly become the basis for centralized power. If the latter emerges it would have to be through prophets. If the Nuer are anything to go by, such prophets are drawn from this sort of penumbra of freakish people at the margins of society.

I'm convinced this connection between domination, care, and monstrosity (in the moral, social, physical, sexual sense) runs far deeper. In fact I'm increasingly convinced this is the real secret of how humans came to lose their most precious freedoms, how we end up with real fascism.

I'm also coming to think you're right that there's a kind of fascism already inherent in the way we humans appropriate nature. Perhaps that's what my old teacher Marshall Sahlins is really identifying when he now talks about the "Original Political Society" as being an authoritarian state, but one where the rulers are all gods and spirits and other "meta-humans." Hunter-gatherers, he notes, really do live in states if they insist they have arbitrary powers to impose laws and punish transgressions. But I would add: when it hits the human level, they tend to make a comedy of it. There are plenty of societies where the principle of sovereignty doesn't exist in everyday affairs—that is, if you define sovereignty as the ability to give orders backed up by the threat of force, with impunity, to stand outside the system of law and morality in order to be able to claim you constitute it. (That's why sacred kings always have to take power through some great crime, to show that they aren't subject to human laws and are therefore capable of creating them.) No one can give arbitrary orders at all—or at least, you can give all the orders you like, but no one is obliged to pay any attention. Except during rituals. And these rituals involve masked or costumed god impersonators, so you might say "Aha! It's when the divine rulers come to earth, and humans claim to embody them, that you have the origin of kingship and the state." But in fact it's not so simple. If you look at the Kuksu cults in indigenous California, or the masquerades of Tierra del Fuego, what you find is the gods don't say anything: they are impassive; they just exist. The figures who impose order are the clowns. They are at once the masters of the ceremony and powers in their own right, but they're also constantly making fun of the rituals, doing everything backwards or in a ridiculous way to crack people up (and if you laugh, you have to pay money). They can order anyone to stand on their head or sing a song and then fine or punish them if they refuse. They represent sovereignty. But they're ridiculous.

Among the Kwakiutl, you even have clown police, the fool dancers, who officiate over the midwinter ceremonies and can beat or even (supposedly) kill you for making a mistake in the protocol, but who break all the rules themselves and wander around wearing masks with giant noses that they're constantly blowing, and they go nuts if anyone touches them, start throwing rocks and smashing things. But they only exist for three months a year, when all the important people are engaged in ritual masquerades. Those who are actually impersonating gods don't speak. Many, like the cannibal spirit, are overwhelmed by divine afflatus and rendered inarticulate creatures of pure desire. So who exactly are the clowns? Well, one interpretation, my favorite, is that they aren't humans impersonating gods but gods impersonating humans. Or humans impersonating gods impersonating humans. That's why they're so clumsy and idiotic and obsessed with sex and excrement. Because that's what humans look like if you're a god. It casts the deformed princes and princesses of the Ice Age in a new light, certainly.

Then there's the transformation of care into relations of domination, cruelty, and power. Kings are by definition a little like children. This is all very explicit where I was in Madagascar, where in the 19th century they talked of the people as "nurse-maids" of the king—or usually then it was a queen, Ranavalona, always referred to as the "little girl"—which of course makes perfect sense, since monarchs are egotistical, petulant, willful, but entirely dependent on you, just like small children. The entire kingdom was an elaborate system of caring labor attending to the needs and desires—ultimately, the absolute freedom—of the queen.

It was exactly the reverse of what we sometimes now call the "nanny state." But there's a kind of constant slippage, a vibration even, back in forth between the two. There's a constituent relationship between the sovereign and the freakish: the crippled, the mad, deformed, orphaned, runaways, who are alternately, or even simultaneously, seen as being especially sacred and especially profane. That slippage is always talking place. Franz Steiner, for instance, demonstrated how in many free societies (I prefer this term to "egalitarian" or "simple" or "primitive" societies) there's a headman with a great central house, and this is the guest house for travelers but also a refuge for everyone with no other place to go. So widows and orphans and the disabled, runaways from other villages, fleeing crimes or feuds or some other kind of trouble looking for sanctuary, accumulate there, to be taken care of. But the young men, often criminals, can become a kind of strong-arm force and the basis of a kind of punitive power. The Shilluk king comes to be surrounded by a coterie of thugs with nowhere else to go. Or it can flip the other way: charity can flip to slavery.

In Mesopotamia temples would take in women who were orphaned or disabled or otherwise had no one to support them or no place else to go. They'd feed them and care for them and give them wool to spin or cloth to weave. Such temples become the basis for what were arguably the first factories. But then when cities became more warlike and brought home prisoners, they were deposited in the temples too, and the whole labor force turned into slaves. The origins of prostitution—which, incidentally, is not at all the oldest profession—might be the product of a similar process. What are called "temple prostitutes" were at first often the very highest ranked women in society. They were wives of the god. Some were totally celibate, while others officiated and took part in sexual rituals of various kinds. But gradually as farmers fell into debt, money lenders (who were often priests or at least worked in the temple administration) would take away their daughters and sons as debt peons, and many were placed in the temples as more commercialized versions of the same thing. Red light districts started springing up around the sacred places. So the "temple prostitutes" were alternately the highest or lowest in society. One of the most interesting things about the rise of patriarchal religions—which in some ways were the creation of those who fled to the desert to protect their children from being taken away—is the horrified rejection of that system. Which is the outrage and disgust they exhibit when they talk about "Babylon" as the place of money, but therefore also the place of whores.

**MBK:** This is a very profound question that you ask, inasmuch as all the sexual techniques existing in the human being are imitations of the reproductive act. They isolate the most vital aspect of the thing, which is enjoyment, hoping to get rid of the deadly aspect. In reality this aspect is increased, and this is what Freud called the death drive. This is why there's no bulimia or anorexia in animals. The human animal's imitation of primary biological processes, nutrition and sexuality, results in both excesses of all kinds and lacks of all kinds, in enjoyments that did not exist before these imitations, but also in sufferings that arise with them. It's this general process that I try to describe through the concept of pleonectics.

**DG:** I think you would find the Sumerian material telling—that is, if you're not familiar with it already. Of course a lot of it is fragmentary and reconstructed. But it's very clear that the general situation of women declines steadily during the entire period for which we have records. We don't know, but have some reason to believe, that in earlier Neolithic times, women might even have been socially predominant. But during that early time procreative sex was considered profane, even animalistic, for exactly the reason that that's what animals do. Oral, anal, any other non-procreative form of sex was considered divine, precisely because it was the pursuit of pleasure for its own sake (as a form of play or freedom, if you like) which animals don't do. I'm guessing that even the celibacy of some high priestesses was seen as a parallel form of non-procreative sexual excess.

What you're saying, then, if I understand you correctly, is that the separation of sexual pleasure from procreation, which makes it an abstraction, allows it to be endlessly multiplied—that's pleonexia. Yet it's precisely that excess that leads to (among other things presumably) commercialization, and to the puritanical patriarchal reaction, the mortification of the flesh, the obsession with virginity, honor killing, sequestration, ultimately the idea that only procreative sex is permissible—which comes from the exact same region. All these puritanical practices are sex games too, of course. But far darker, more cruel, more violent.

## Leave, disobey, reshuffle

**ATZ:** We've talked about slippage a lot, between different value systems, different distributions of power and social organizations and the *play* necessary to the turnover process between them.

**DG:** Yes, for most of human history, these terms were unstable, and in flux, and in a way that instability was precisely what freedom consisted of. Or at least a case can be made that it was.

As I think I mentioned, when David Wengrow and I started writing our book, we rapidly concluded that "the origins of inequality" is rather a foolish problem. In fact, speaking of "inequality" as a uniform factor in human society, one you can measure by the same Gini coefficient from the Ice Age to the present, is downright bizarre.

There are so many better ways to frame what's wrong with the world: capitalism, patriarchy, class power, exploitation, domination ... Focusing instead on "inequality" pretty much assumes a liberal technocratic approach to solving global problems— well, we'll just tinker a bit with income rates; half-measures are obviously required since we wouldn't want everyone to have exactly the same thing. That would be crazy and totalitarian. The problem, we concluded, was not that some people have more stuff, but that they can turn wealth into power, to make people to do things they would otherwise not wish to do, or create a world where some people are told their needs and perspectives don't matter.

One reason "origins of inequality" fables make sense to us is because the image we have caught in our heads of what hunter-gatherers—and by implication all primordial humans—are like are the Mbuti, the pygmies of Central Africa, the Bushmen of the Kalahari desert, or maybe the East African Hadza. They all live in tiny egalitarian bands. But such people are not really typical of hunter-gatherers historically. It's just that in 1901—when Franz Boas was carrying out his research on the Northwest Coast or Baldwin Spencer in Australia, where people lived very differently—anthropologists weren't yet in the habit of following people around with stop-watches, timing their daily calorie intake, and documenting everything on film. By the time "modern scientific methods" came in, the only hunter-gatherers left were tiny populations, often refugee populations, living in places no one else wanted—deserts, tundra, etc. And there were movies, celebrity informants like Nai and Nisa, all this made a huge impression. Everyone decided this must be what 95% of human history was really like. This is the period a lot of anarchists began insisting that "civilization" was a terrible mistake and we should all go back to being hunter-gatherers, usually side-stepping or finessing the point (which they'd acknowledge among themselves) that 99.9% of the current population of the planet would have to die—which of course raised certain questions about who the "we" was supposed to be. It was basically a politics of hopelessness—let's just throw everything away; it's all going to come crashing down anyway...

So we started asking, what were arrangements—particularly political arrangements—really like for most of human history? We can't really know much about what was happening, say, two hundred thousand years ago—that period is basically a kind of shadow screen on which people throw their mythological fantasies—but if you start with, say, the Ice Age, then compare with the ethnographic record... Well, one remarkable thing is that people would completely change their social structures over the course of the year.

There's is a wonderful little book by Marcel Mauss, *Seasonal Variations of the Eskimo*, which describes this kind of "dual morphology," as he calls it. In the summer the Inuit would disperse into little patriarchal bands, and had strict rules of private property and were sexually puritan. But in the winter they gathered together in micro-cities. There'd be communal property arrangements; they'd have great wife-swapping orgies under the aegis of Sedna, Mistress of the Seals... There was a completely different social structure in different times of year. This was extremely common. The people Boas studied, to their immediate south, literally had different names in different times of the year. They'd literally become someone else (one role of the clown police was to punish people for using their summer names in winter).

All this meant that people were keenly aware that social structure wasn't something immutable. You can change it around—which meant people were actually far *more* politically self-aware than we are.

Stonehenge is another example! The people who built Stonehenge were former cereal farmers who gave up raising cereal and went back to gathering nuts (though they kept the domestic animals). This appears to have happened across the entirety of what is now the British Isles, and I always wondered, how did people back then coordinate this sort of thing? The British Isles aren't a small place. But apparently around 3000 bc there was some mechanism by which everyone made a collective decision to stop growing grain. Well, one thing we do know is that the people who lived near Stonehenge only lived there three months a year. People—some of whom normally lived quite far away—would stay there, perform midwinter rituals around their giant monument, during which time they apparently had a king. Then they scattered back into tiny bands for the rest of the year with their animals, living literally on nuts and berries. Presumably during that time the royals lived pretty much like anyone else. The kingdom was assembled and dismantled yearly. Which is presumably how you have all these Frazerian myths about kings who are killed or sacrificed on an annual basis. It seems to me the very ability to shift back and forth between social structures like that was what made it seem plausible to people that you could just rearrange everything—adopt farming, give up farming—on a level it would never occur to us to be able to do today.

If this is true, the question we needed to ask was not "Where did social inequality come from?" but "How did we get stuck in a situation where we can't disassemble this when it no longer suits our purposes?"

There's a little bit of that left over in festivals. Mayday, which was the British equivalent of carnival, when you would try on alternative social structures, was the starting point of most British peasant revolts. But it's just a shadow of earlier arrangements.

**ATZ:** Which of course raises the question of how we get "stuck" in a fixed structure.

**DG:** And in a way being "stuck" has an even broader meaning: it means being stuck in one place, stuck in one structure, finally stuck in relations of domination which you can't simply flee or ignore.

One obvious question is if we ditch the phrase "egalitarian" or "egalitarian society," how do we talk about the qualities we admire in so many stateless or indigenous societies? What is it that Mbuti and Jivaro and Stonehenge Britons had in common (assuming they had anything in common)? I have been coming around to simply talking of "free societies." It strikes me that, whether or not there were formal political offices, or formal separation of men and women, and so forth... well, if there's something we humans really have *lost*, over time, it's certain freedoms that were once simply assumed and now seem so exotic we can hardly imagine them.

I would list three primordial freedoms of this sort, just provisionally (it's possible the list can be expanded and refined.) First: freedom to leave. Which is also freedom to travel. Often a significant proportion of the people living in, say, a hunter-gatherer band, come from someplace far away. We have this odd idea that in "primitive times," any stranger would be assumed to be an enemy and probably killed. In fact, in most times and places there were elaborate rules of hospitality, so anywhere you went in North America you could find fellow members of the bear clan, and anywhere you went in Australia people of the same moiety, who would be obliged to put you up. At first, at least, there was no mechanism for excluding people who wished to simply move (though much later, in many places, this changes—another example of the double-sidedness of care, and as we all know "host," "hostage," and "hostile" are all etymologically related). So if everyone has the freedom to leave, there are acute limits on creating abusive social relations.

I remember reading a conversation between some anthropologist and a friend from Papua New Guinea who was visiting America, and he was asking if he admired American freedoms. And his friend said "To be honest I think we have more at home. Look at that hill over there, maybe five miles away. Back home, if I saw a hill and wanted to see what it was like on top, I could just walk there and climb the hill. Here there are a thousand reasons why I wouldn't be allowed to."

It might seem a little odd to describe the freedom to go elsewhere as a form of freedom, as a right, at all, because no one in most of the societies where it exists really talks about it that way. We use the language; we talk about the right to freedom of movement. But for the most part this language is illusory, since the legal right to go to, say, Malaysia, let alone to go from Malaysia to Europe or America, means nothing if you can't afford the flight. A lot of migrants end up in debt for the rest of their lives and atrocious things result. Those societies that genuinely have freedom of movement don't use that language at all but instead speak of it as "the responsibility of hospitality." Your obligation to take care of strangers, of course, seen from another point of view, is precisely your own freedom to travel.

The second freedom is the freedom to ignore orders. This is perhaps the most important. All human languages have an imperative form, a way to say "stand up" or "sit down," but for most of human history those inclined to give orders didn't have any means of compelling you to stand up or sit down should you decide not to do so. People will say "Kondiaronk didn't come from an egalitarian society—the Wendat had a whole system of political offices, and he himself was effectively foreign minister..." And all this was quite true, but he had no power to compel anyone to do anything they didn't want to do. The Jesuits were always talking about this, how the Indians kept teasing them because they were afraid of their superiors, while, they would say "We laugh and make sport of ours." This is what made them a free people. (It's also why political figures like Kondiaronk had to be so persuasive.)

Interestingly, they saw a certain "baseline communism," as I'd call it, a certain expectation of mutual aid, as one element of that insistence on absolute personal autonomy, since you aren't free to do much of anything if you're a beggar on the street. In fact, you could easily end up in a situation where you can't refuse orders.

This is why many feminist anthropologists prefer not to speak of women's equality but rather women's "autonomy." The question isn't equality of status—which it's unclear what that even means in many societies where men and women largely have bemused contempt for one another—but rather whether men are in a position, individually or collectively, of telling women what to do, or interfering with their projects.

So we have the freedom to go elsewhere and the freedom to ignore commands. I would say the third freedom is the freedom to reshuffle the social order entirely, seasonally or otherwise. But as I say, seasonal shifts make it much easier to imagine this. This is why the Osage could so impress Montesquieu.

So in that sense we've gotten stuck in at least three different ways.

**ATZ:** And so how? It seems to have something to do with the annihilating power of capitalism's representation.

**DG:** Well it happened long before capitalism. But sure, you can say that capitalism is the highest form of whatever it is that was stuck. Even if it typically represents itself as the opposite.

**ATZ:** So when do we start to enact our representations to such a degree that we no longer remember how to opt out of them?

**DG:** That's an interesting thought. Do you think that's what happened? Let's see.

If you look for examples of when representations outrace reality, or when misrepresentations become powerful and start reorganizing society around them, they're not that hard to find. Four examples come to mind right away.

One thing I noticed a long time ago, but never knew what to do with, was the fact that when medieval authors wrote about politics they almost always assume something like a nation state, even where nothing remotely like one existed. Most of Europe at the time… what you actually have are incredibly complex checkerboards of different sorts of overlapping sovereignty, but if you read a medieval Romance, or fairytale, or some theorist talking about the nature of politics in theoretical terms, they always assume a single prince with power over a unified territory.

It's the same with slavery. Even though in reality you have endless gradations of vassalage, service, when anyone starts talking about such matters in the abstract they tend to speak of masters and slaves. They talk about power as if it were an incredibly simple unitary thing and ignore lived experience, where it's infinitely subtle and everyone is negotiating the terms of hierarchy all the time.

A third example has to do with… well, pleonexia again. Everybody presumes it. Or to be more precise everyone presumes the Augustinian conception of human nature as incorrigible—that we're creatures of infinite desire, that this was our punishment for disobeying God, and for this reason we'd all be at war with one another or eating each other like fish weren't for the strong hand of the law. In the Middle Ages everybody read Augustine, who makes this argument, but it's not like anyone really *acted* that way. It's particular dramatic in the economic sphere. Almost no one pursued open-ended projects of accumulation. As in most times and places, most people, even merchants, operated with target incomes. They had a conception of what it would take to achieve the "good life," and if they got it, they'd stop working and "maximize leisure time," as an economist would put it, so as to actually enjoy that good life. Even if they all also subscribed to a theology that said they shouldn't. Obviously, at some point some people started actually enacting the Augustinian theory in practice. One may ask why. Weber suggested it had something to do with Calvinism: the restless anxiety about salvation, the feeling it was sinful to enjoy life. Gradually such sensibilities spread, though never to everyone. (This is the reason it's so hard to get a taxi in the rain, incidentally. Cab drivers tend to work with target incomes, and when they make enough money, which they do very quickly if it's raining, they tend to just go home.)

Finally, I think there's a fourth example, though less medieval. I remember reading an essay by Pierre Bourdieu where he points out that if you look at the theory of the bureaucratic state to be found in Marx, or Durkheim, or Weber, at the time of writing they basically got it wrong. However, over time their theories became increasingly true, largely because everyone who's actually running a bureaucratic system has taken courses in university where they're forced to read Marx, Durkheim, and Weber.

So that's sovereignty, domination, pleonexia, bureaucracy... oh, there's a fifth! Private property. That might be another example. One of the things that always strikes me about living in England is how weird the property regime is. No one really knows who the land belongs to. There are apparently five or six dukes and barons who "really" own all of London, but there are still four or five different claimants with different sorts of rights in every building. There's leasehold, copyhold, freehold, all sorts of rules left over from feudal tenure. And I remember thinking once, "Wait a minute! Isn't England supposed to be the first home of possessive individualism, of modern private-property rights held 'against all the world,' where people came to reimagine their rights and obligations to one another entirely in terms of exclusive property rights?" There are no exclusive property rights in England! Even now. *Maybe* Scotland. But really not even there. So the relation of representation and practice is very different from what we imagine in very practical ways.

So the question: Did simplified representation eventually invade the complex practice? Or does it just provide a template one might appeal to over the course of some social struggle? Marshall Sahlins of course argues that the entire science of economics is just a secularized version of medieval theology, with some of the terms reversed. In that case the simplified representation won. But the British landed gentry, by contrast, have largely been able to resist a similar simplification of land tenure.

# Great man theory and historical necessity

**ATZ:** On my way here I was reading a special issue of a newspaper that proposed to span history's great thinkers. The way these people—well, men—are discussed is an important part of the way "revolutions in common sense" are memorialized. I couldn't really get through any section past the thinkers that were remembered as one person but may very well have been many. After that you get this messianic tone that, say, Heidegger had this one completely original thought that we'd all ignorantly been waiting for.

**DG:** Well one of the great mysteries of human life to me is the fact that once a historical event happens you can't say whether it had to happen or what would have been different had it not happened. Would the same thing have happened in a different place two weeks later?

**ATZ:** Right and then there is this: I was born in a pool in which all of this thought has already occurred, all of this already exists. To try and unravel it chronologically and individually to each philosopher is interesting for general culture purposes, but makes me feel as though I'm trying to "un-dissolve" or "re-dissociate" things that today appear to be common sense. In the same way that when my father puts the Rolling Stones on and says "We had never heard anything like this Assia!" I just can't fathom that.

**DG:** And for people who have heard the Rolling Stones all their lives, you listen to most of what passed as pop music in the 50s and you just can't conceive of how anyone could possibly have enjoyed it.

**MBK:** The temporality of philosophy is very special. I always explain something very simple: to drive a car you don't need to be a mechanic and to use concepts you don't have to know or read philosophy. The concept of "idea" was invented by Plato two and a half thousand years ago, but you don't need to know that now to have one. Most people today use the concept of capitalism without having read Marx, and same goes for Freud and the ego.

**DG:** So philosophy has been able to create a series of global revolutions in Wallerstein's sense of transformations of common sense. The obvious question then is: was the person the event, or did the event produce the person? We can't know. Marx is a wonderful example because many Marxists will insist his work disproved the "great men theory of history," but with one exception ... [*chuckles*]

**MBK:** Which is?

**DG:** Marx! "One man single-handedly showed us that one man can't change the course of history?" How does that make any sense? So I always wonder whether from a Marxist point of view the birth of Marx was a historical necessity.

**MBK:** That's the vertiginous question about what an event is.

**ATZ:** David, you spoke about prophets, sovereigns, and madmen. So perhaps we've come to the question of prophets.

**DG:** That's very relevant to the question of Marx. I was saying that the Nuer have this sort of penumbra of potential prophets, people who are considered mad or at least very strange. They spend their days arranging shells and talking to themselves, and mostly people just ignore them, but the moment there's a great catastrophe, a plague, the danger of generalized warfare, an alien invasion, these are the people they turn to to resolve problems larger than the local community. So you wonder was Marx—and people like him—the equivalent? Had history gone in a different direction, would he have been some eccentric journalist who took part in some crazy political group which had eight members? Or maybe an author of children's books? Or alternatively, had Marx gotten hit by a carriage or died of scarlet fever at age three, would some person that we remember as a children's book writer have risen to the occasion? How different would his theories have been? Would he have to have been German, or could he have been an Indian postman or a schoolteacher in Nigeria? That's the great unknown. Social theorists aren't allowed to ask such questions. It's almost a kind of taboo, so it's relegated to speculative fiction. To be considered professional, social scientists must speak of events that have already happened in a way that suggests they were entirely inevitable, and by implication predictable—despite the fact that of course when we do try to predict events we almost invariably get it wrong.

**MBK:** My question is very simple: what about the future?

**DG:** Well, one reason I spend so much time re-writing the past is because I am convinced it's currently being written the way it is so as to make it almost impossible for us to imagine a viable future. That's why I annoy everyone by insisting that communism already exists. One thing we learnt in Zuccotti Park during Occupy is that Americans are actually quite good at communism. They're just not very good at democracy. That, they have to be taught. Obviously this is not at all Americans' self-conception. In a similar way I think that we've written history in such a way that social movements basically don't exist until the Enlightenment. After the philosophers clarify that historical agency is possible, then suddenly revolutions begin to take place. This is not only silly, it's also very boring, because it means you have to have the same arguments about the Krondstadt or the Paris Commune or Barcelona in 1936 over and over and over again. Finally it's depressing, because it means revolutions, "real" revolutions have only been possible for a few hundred years, and even during that time they almost invariably failed. But if you lift the veil of the Enlightenment and say it didn't really introduce anything that shockingly different...

Well, maybe it's no coincidence that the most creative revolutionary movements of the last decades, the Zapatistas in Chiapas and the Kurdish movement in Turkey and Syria, have been ones that see themselves as rooted in very ancient traditions of revolt.

**MBK:** It's a very Walter Benjaminian idea.

**ATZ:** Ah, what would've happened if he hadn't died!

**MBK:** It was an idea that Lacoue-Labarthe express very well, in a quote I'd like to read to you : "It is in a tension between the "very old" (the forgotten) and the "new" or the modern (the coming) that we feel and know how to exist. We do not believe the old liquid nor the modern outdated. We would rather think old and modern as one and the other-together unfinished in the sense that, in the accomplished program of the one and the other, there remains something undone."

You are very close to his thought in two proposi-tions: First, saying that the event doesn't occur ex-nihilo; it's always a conjunction. And second, turn-ing to the past to invent new possibilities.

**DG:** For me, a "post-modern" argument is precisely one that refuses to do this. Say you "suddenly dis-cover" some new aspect of capitalism, say, immate-rial labor. Only a tiny portion of the value of a Nike sneaker is derived from the materials and the labor that went into putting them together. Maybe 95% of it comes from the value of the brand, and that's produced not just by advertisers and marketers, but even more, perhaps, by amateurs, subcultures, hip-hop artists, their fans, kids playing basketball on the street… Well, what do you do with this realization?

You can say "Wait a minute, let's look back at the entire history of capitalism and see if there are things going on we didn't notice before because we didn't realize they were important," like the work women are doing even back in the days of Wedgwood, creating the cultural context of commodities. Or you can say "Clearly, the world changed completely in 1975, and the labor theory of value no longer applies"—and refuse to do that retrospective work.

In a sense, then, you could even say that post-modernism is a refusal of the logic of the event. If a true event reorganizes your sense of reality so that everything, including history, looks different—it "allows you to see", as Assia nicely put it, aspects of reality you would never have previously noticed or even been able to imagine—then the post-modern move is a refusal to do so. What you take to be an event is just a rupture. Nothing more. It implies a kind of giddy presentism which simulates radicalism, but is in fact the death of politics.

This is what I was trying to do with social movements. Kondiaronk, the Wendat statesman who so inspires the Enlightenment thinkers of the next generations—it turns out he didn't just *happen* either! If you look at the history of North America, there was an urban civilization centered on what's now East St. Louis, around one thousand ad. It's called Cahokia. We don't really understand well what was happening there, but it much resembles Meso-american empires, apparently with some kind of caste system, hereditary priesthood, human sacrifice. There's evidence of quite brutal goings-on, but then suddenly it all collapses. Whatever happened, the place wasn't remembered fondly. For centuries, the heartland of the old empire was entirely abandoned. It was sort of like the forbidden zone in *Planet of the Apes*—no one lived there. Cahokia is at first replaced by smaller kingdoms, but they

also collapse. A few generations later European settlers show up and find these fiercely independent
people living in polis-sized tribal republics, smoking tobacco, drinking caffeinated beverages, hanging around in the public square arguing about politics all day. Some are rationalists, even Freudians,
some of them are nature-loving hippies; many, like
the Cherokee, even have myths saying "Well there
used to be these hereditary priests who pushed us
around, raped women, did bad things, so we killed
those guys, and since then we reject the principle
of formal priesthood or hereditary leadership." I
mean they didn't make a secret of what happened.
Yet somehow the settlers couldn't accept it and to
this day most historians just assume the indigenous
peoples of the Eastern Woodlands were just somehow like that and always had been. Whereas clearly
there had been social movements, presumably of
any number of different kinds, and that anti-cler-
ical skeptical rationalism that so struck men like
Lahontan was itself the product of a long history
of political contention. It was then imported and
found conducive by thinkers in Europe (along with
tobacco and the habit of arguing about politics over
caffeinated beverages). Yet we somehow blinded
ourselves to this. So the Enlightenment itself comes
out of earlier social movements, and yet its legacy is
that we have convinced ourselves that prior to the
Enlightenment nobody could've had a self-aware
movement.

**MBK:** Globalization also raises the question of redis-
covering the past for what is present. What is new
is the ability to re-create the past into a manifold

humanity. It's a question of survival. Philosophers fifty years ago didn't have the knowledge necessary to affirm this.

**DG:** To affirm what?

**MBK:** That capitalism is suicide. When you study other possibilities of life in the Amazon, it's not simply to say "Let's live like that." It's to say something very precise about the world, about this very abstract yet concrete unification of our world under capitalism which leads us not only to this horrible life we experience but to the suicide of the species. It's very important in my work to explain this acceleration.

**DG:** I've thought about this as well, the way people talk about the "direction of history." While it's silly to look at most of history as if it's going in one direction, reason really wasn't *that* cunning. One thing globalization means is that it's now possible to create a history that goes in one direction, which was not the case before. So we brought about a situation where that which we had previously projected incorrectly onto the past now becomes possibly true in the future.

**ATZ:** Which again is just our representations being caught up with by our experiences.

**DG:** That's true! Of course the direction we seem to have taken for now is catastrophic, but it opens the possibility of choosing other ones.

**MBK:** My interpretation of anarchy is the deconstruction of the unification of representation through capitalistic ideology. It's like the idea of God. It was here to save us and does absolutely the opposite. The idea of deconstructing this unity of capitalism is to invent the manifold. When you show us different ways of living it is to invent the present and the future.

**ATZ:** Right, but I don't think we need so much to *invent* the manifold as encourage it where it already exists. Anthropology, done right anyway, teaches us that the great unification is never as successful as it imagines itself to be in the first place. Acknowledging this would mean that we put an end to the representation that makes the actual lived multiplicities suffer for being "monstrous" surplus products. In this way I find there to be a redemptive power in anthropology, coming to the awareness of the possibility of plurality that already exists.

## Theories of desire

**ATZ:** You've written about desire in your piece on consumption, which was very important to me. And pleonexia of course is also about desire… Can we talk a bit about theories of desire?

**DG:** Well, if you like. I always worry mine were crude. I was trying to understand the differences between two broad conceptions: Plato's hunger model of desire—"desire as lack," or the negation of a negation, which one might say opens the way to the theological view of the human condition as one of incorrigible beings in a universe of scarcity—and the more optimistic conception of "life which desires itself," the Spinozan vitalist tradition, which you could say ultimately sees desire as freedom and play, the expression of life's full capacities for their own sake. It's obvious why the latter seems more appealing, but it strikes me that either can lead to some Hobbesian war of all against all, one more economistic, the other perhaps more fascistic.

Where do you want to go from that?

**ATZ:** To follow the intuition that re-tracing a history of desire would mean re-considering theories of value?

**DG:** Aha! That's ambitious. But worthwhile.

Okay, let's give it a whirl.

The essay was specifically about the notion of "consumption," how advocates of theories of what came to be known as "creative consumption" show up in the 80s and basically bully their way into dominance. It's quite subtle, as it arrives claiming to be a critique, but a very insidious one that in reality institutes the thing it is ostensibly criticizing.

This corresponds to a certain moment in capitalism of "market segmentation." Basically, advertisers and marketers stop trying to create a homogeneous consumer public and start breaking down the public into identity groups (strivers, makers, survivors... they had endless categories) and coming up with specific strategies to target them. All these people are getting rich selling each other "bibles" breaking down postal codes or telephone area codes by supposed consumer orientation. Partly as a result, marketers stop just hiring psychologists (and it was already the case in the US that most psychologists were working for advertisers and not in universities) and start hiring more people with anthropological training. And lo and behold, within the discipline itself, there's this curious moral transformation: all cultures are defined as subcultures, and all subcultures, as countercultures, as forms of resistance. Endless articles come out chiding anthropologists for downplaying consumption.

The line you hear repeated over and over again is "We used to talk about consumption in this very naïve Frankfurt School style whereby capitalism produces demand and desires through artificial stimulation, but now we realize that consumption is actually a form of subversive self-expression. If you really take working-class people seriously, they love their cars and motorcycles and leather jackets." But of course the joke is we didn't "used to talk about consumption" at all. I can't think of a single anthropological article from the 70s that applied a Frankfurt School approach to consumption. Anthropologists wrote about clothing, or food, houses, parties, and so forth, but not as things people "consume." In fact the critics were importing the notion of consumption into a discourse where it never was before! They were re-inserting the terms of political economy whilst pretending to critique the way that political economy is done. What I started to ask was why consumption? Not just "Why do we suddenly have to act like if a woman in Trinidad puts on a crazy costume for carnival, what's really important here is that someone manufactured the beads and the cloth," but also "Why do we suddenly have to imagine our relationship to the material world, to pleasure and enjoyment, primarily through the metaphor of eating food?"

After all, you could just as easily see what we call "consumption" as the product of people and social relations, or a dozen other ways. So that's why I felt I had to take on theories of desire. I had just read a book by a sociologist named Colin Campbell called *The Romantic Ethic and the Spirit of Modern Consumerism*, where he made the argument that what capitalism is really selling people is daydreams. There are material limits, he argued, to the degree to which you expand traditional hedonism: food, sex, drugs, music (wine, women, and song; sex and drugs and rock 'n' roll, or whatever the local variant). There's only so much of it you can really experience before you get bored and sated; also there are logistical problems. Capitalism, however, has to expand infinitely.

Now, the funny thing here is that Campbell doesn't actually have a problem with this; he's one of those one-time 60s rebels who's settled into his comfy academic job and wants to convince himself that all that old anti-consumerist rhetoric was naive. So he says "Well, the standard critique used to be that capitalism presents us with fantasies, i.e. if I only get this dress, or this car, or this toothpaste, my life will be transformed, I will be beautiful and everyone will love me or at least want to have sex with me. Then of course you get the object and you're invariably disappointed. This, critics often point out, is a classic depressive pattern and seems to be the reason why rates of clinic depression always go up in prosperous, consumer societies." Well, Campbell says these critics miss the point. What capitalism is really selling you is, precisely, the fantasies. In fact advertising, publicity, marketing are giant engines for producing daydreams—or material for daydreams, "modern self-illusory hedonism" as he puts it—which can indeed be expanded infinitely.

So that was an entertaining premise, and it inspired me to start looking at theories of desire— but as soon as I did, I realized Campbell was not just wrong, he had it completely backwards. One need only look at medieval theories of desire and the imagination—the ones documented by Agamben and Couliano—which appear to go back to Arabic medical literature and become the basis for much medieval ceremonial magic (and I would argue, through it, modern advertising techniques as well, since these are often just elaborations of techniques pioneered by occultists like Giordano Bruno). Well, they just assumed that the proper object of desire was an image, a phantasm, rather than a material object. This is partly because their model for desire was erotic attraction. Obviously, they said, the real pleasure was in yearning, anticipation, fantasy; when you obtain the object, it will almost certainly disappoint, at least eventually. Those obsessed by the idea that they could resolve the problem by actually seizing and embracing the material object were entirely missing the point that this was itself a species of melancholia. So from the perspective of medieval psychology, consumer capitalism actually *would* be a gigantic example of clinical depression.

So why our obsession not with sex but with food as the model for desire? Actually, I found Agamben helpful here too, in an entirely different way. He noted that sovereignty is typically conceived as the power of life and death, and in fact, even today, "life" has little meaning outside it. We say things are alive, basically, because we can kill them. It occurred to me that doesn't this point to a paradox within our idea of private property as well? Because both are defined in medieval terms as a species of *dominium*, as I've already pointed out, they are sort of the same thing. In Roman law you have three rights over your property: *usus*, *fructus*, and *abusus*, the right to use, to enjoy the fruits of, and to damage or destroy an object. If you just have the former two, you have usufruct; it's not really yours. But that means what makes property really yours is your right to destroy it, in much the same way as a king knows someone is really his subject because he can kill him.

(You can see how this is totally consistent with what I was saying earlier, that the paradigmatic form of property is actually a person, a slave. Roman owners were able to kill slaves with impunity, which in most legal traditions is the one line they're not supposed to cross.)

So far so good. This does help resolve some of the paradoxes of private property we were been talking about earlier, but it introduces another one: the only way to absolutely prove something is yours, that you absolutely have it, is to destroy it. But then of course you don't have it any more. So how do you overcome the paradox? Well, the answer is obvious. You can eat it. It's the only way to destroy something and still have it at the same time.

**ATZ:** Wow, so we'd need to come up with tantric models of consumption!

**DG:** Ok, I am putting you in charge of that.

**MBK:** To put in a provocative way, in the book with Jean-Luc Nancy on sexuality we raise the question of prostitution, which is a kind of immediate sexual consumption. And I ask Jean Luc the question of abstract desire, why a prostitute can never have the prestige they did in Sumer? Why is Sasha Grey, a pornographic actress who reads Nietzsche and listens to Joy Division, not praised when stupid top models are?

**ATZ:** Well, you don't know that the top models are stupid.
But I guess it's simply because we hate the one that kills abstract desire by materializing it. We dream of the models becoming porn stars, and we like them because they don't.

**MBK:** Yes, but for me it's still a speculative mystery.

**DG:** I've always liked Baudrillard's point that what fascinates is above all what radically excludes us in the name of its own inner logic or perfection: cats, narcissists, paranoid systems... A fashion model doesn't need you. But I guess I'm just restating Assia's point.
All this makes me think about what you once wrote, Mehdi, about Deleuze and sado-masochism. What Deleuze gives is an ontology of desire, but where the desire is unfulfilled. At least that's true of

the male masochist; realization, orgasm, is endlessly suspended. And of course, that's what was happening in the medieval concept of romantic love as well. The beloved is a kind of dominatrix, testing and tormenting you, and you're supposed to get off on the frustration and never achieve release, or at least not admit to it—well, for obvious reasons, since we're almost necessarily talking about relations outside marriage here. You make the very nice point that if desire is reality, then realization is not making real (the literal meaning of the term), but the very opposite. Orgasm is annihilation; it ends everything. I found this remarkable not least because it synthesizes the two theories: desire as lack and desire as life.

**ATZ:** Interesting that you reconcile them so well, because I was about to take issue with this distinction as anything other than a cycle or a dialectic, not life *or* lack but life-lack-life. The same way it isn't really life and death, but cycles of life death life. The depression-inducing factor is just the shortsightedness of the vision, mostly chronically the male vision.

**MBK:** That makes me think about my central question in my *Système du pléonectique*: the question of unlimited desire. We have to learn from imitation; in sadomasochism what interests me are techniques of imitation. Freud's discovery, and thus the reason why it is only in humans that there is an unconscious mind, is that the difference between a drive and an instinct is precisely this question of imitation. You have neither gluttony nor anorexia in animals. When you imitate the animal process of nutrition and sexuality, you do it without imitating the death part.

**DG:** Which means it comes back at you in some even more excessive form.

I'll will be honest and say that Mehdi's work is a real challenge to me. I'm a student of Marshall Sahlins, so I was trained to see unlimited desire as a theological illusion. Marshall always insisted the trouble with what we have come to call Western civilization is that it was founded on a false idea of human nature that traces back to the Sophists perhaps, through the Christian fathers' conception of original sin, to liberal economists' conception of utility. It has only been in relatively recent times that any appreciable number of people in the world really began acting this way. Your work is a remarkably powerful secular theology that embraces the idea of original sin, not sin against God—in fact, if I understand you correctly, the project of creating God was an intrinsic part of the sin. So economic pleonectics is just one particular manifestation of a more fundamental aspect of what made us human, and which is now in the process of destroying the planet.

What you appear to be asking is: is there something inherent to the nature of human appropriation of nature ("techno-mimetic appropriation," as you put it) that means that all societies are haunted by at least the potential for this kind of runaway excess, this demonic aspect of human desire.

Well, a case could surely be made.

As I've noted, it's often the most peaceful, egalitarian societies that are most inclined to surround themselves with phantasmal visions of horror: the creation of the universe is generally to seen to be an ugly business of monstrous sex, shit, projectile vomiting, entirely excessive trickster gods, the violation of all boundaries; the cosmic forces battling it out around them are violently insane. So yes, it's as if those who have their own house in order are so because they are keenly aware of pleonectic dangers. Do they also see such dangers as connected to the human capacity for techniques of imitation, the way you talk about human life as a parody of nature? This is trickier. There are cases where something like that is clearly going on. One of my favorite examples is the Piaroa, whose ethnographer, Joanna Overing, describes as masters of the art of getting along. People who put enormous thought (and playful humor) into ensuring peace and individual freedom, good-natured indulgence of idiosyncrasy. But they are also convinced that the techniques of civilization, the culinary arts, weaving, medicine, were invented by evil cannibalistic buffoons at the beginning of time, and the knowledge of how to do them has to be conveyed carefully, because it's laced with destructive madness.

**ATZ:** Which is how a lot of worried parents feel about their children leaving to art school, I guess.

## Graeber reads MBK and proposes
## a three-way dialectic that ends in care

**DG:** Still, I do wonder, Mehdi, about one aspect of your formulation of appropriation versus expropriation. Would it not be better to speak of three terms? On the one hand we create this idealized world (of science, metaphysics, politics) which we then imagine generates reality. Because that isn't true; we're left with this monstrous residual, and also with the pleonectic structures of excess, greed, sadism, terror, and suffering. As you observe, none of this really happens with other species. Yet that very creation of terror and suffering also creates endless relations of care, which also don't exist in the animal world.

**MBK:** Yes, it creates love, which is a fantastic thing. But when you are expropriated from love, it's the worst situation possible. So to put it quickly it's a fight, it's not a definitive pessimism.

**DG:** If it were a definitive pessimism I don't suppose we'd have been drawn to each others' work in the first place.

Still, what if we think about it as a three-way dialectic. As you argue in the *Algebra of Tragedy*, techno-mimetic appropriation generation, which makes us human, creates both ideal mathematical world and un-acknowledged underside. That's true, but I'd add that in doing so it also generates an even more invisible layer of love and care, which makes it possible for us to survive regardless.

At some point in the Middle Ages there was a war between the Bulgar empire and the Byzantines. The Byzantine emperor captured 10,000 Bulgarian soldiers and had them systematically blinded. Except every hundredth, who he'd leave with one eye to lead the others back. It was all intended to terrify the Bulgar emperor, who was presumably operating with some principle of aristocratic honor alien to the mass-industrial cruelty typical of true states, and it worked. When the king saw what happened, he had a heart attack and died. This is a perfect example of a kind of massive pleonectic sadism. But typically the story ends with the king's death. What happened after that? Presumably, for every one of those ten thousand blinded warriors, somebody—most likely a woman—had to spend much of the rest of her life taking care of him. Somehow those people always get left out of the history.

What always strikes me about violent atrocity is the inconceivable disparity between cause and effect. It takes two seconds to pop somebody's eye out, or use a hot iron or whatever they did, but the effects last decades. And it takes someone the rest of her life to care for someone who is blind.

## Art and atrocity

**DG:** I also keep thinking about Mehdi's point—in one of your books, I can't even remember which, now—about art and atrocity: that even in the Middle Ages and Renaissance, artistic themes centered on extraordinary violence; not just battle scenes, but torture (the crucifixion, the flaying of Marsyas), rape (the Sabine women, Leda and the swan) I was thinking about this when visiting the eighteenth-century mansion of some English aristocrat which is now a museum; every table had a little classical-themed bronze or marble statue on it, and I swear at least half of them were rape scenes, or preludes to rape. And I remember thinking, good lord, what kind of person thought these would be nice objects to have around while sipping tea with family friends?

This certainly hasn't been true in all times and places. But it sometimes occurs to me that nowadays the difference between low and high art, or what we're taught we must consider low and high genres, turns the effect on the audience. Go to an expensive gallery, and you'll see works of art that allude to humor, but they're not actually funny. You're definitely not supposed to laugh. There are works that allude to sexuality, but they don't arouse you sexually. Everything is translated into a secondary, cerebral plane. Actual comedy or erotica or horror or porn—even music that you'd actually want to listen to—are considered inferior genres.

So if the work effects you, it's on a much more abstract level. It makes some kind of argument, and you have to assume that any way it startles or amuses or charms you is part of that argument. All this is obvious, I guess. But in a way—and this is less obvious, perhaps—I think this is true of the "low" genres too. They deploy the reaction they invoke as a kind of argument. Take horror movies. Horror is an extremely Christian genre. It's always about transgression and punishment. You do something slightly bad, or stupid, or maybe you're just an obnoxious snotty teenager, so you get eviscerated. The punishment seems entirely disproportionate. Do they really deserve this? But the message seems to be: well, of course they deserve it. They're guilty. Everybody's sinful. Everyone's guilty. Look at yourself. You aren't? If you weren't sinful, why would you be sitting here getting off on this sadistic crap?

So nowadays, where you have high and low genres, high art functions as a kind of divinization of financial abstraction, low art of consumerism. But what about before the industrial revolution, or even capitalism, came on the scene? Perhaps what was really important was establishing the frame itself. Have you ever read Erving Goffman's *Frame Analysis*? He compiles all these hilarious examples of, say, nineteenth-century theatre troupes performing in small towns that have to contend with audience members who keep jumping on stage to disarm actors who pull out a gun. You have to teach people not to do that.

Someone once wrote about rollercoasters (which, by the way, I hate and have always hated—I would like the world to know this) that what they're really about is trust in technology. If you're sitting in a vehicle that's hurdling downwards at an extremely rapid speed, well obviously your natural instinct is to *do* something. But rollercoasters create an artificial situation where you're aware that the only safe thing you can do is absolutely nothing, and the enjoyment lies in completely surrendering your will to the competence of the engineer who designed the ride. The only way you can survive this experience is to not do anything. Perhaps there's something similar in the artistic representations of terrible situations. They also evoke a desire to intervene, but in a situation where it's obviously impossible. Perhaps they're modeling the experience of passivity and teaching it to you.

**MBK:** In the case of tragedy, it's the question of participation. In the examples that David gives in his work, the catharsis is always collective. You always participate, like in tragedy for the Greeks. So when does a form of art like football begin? You've already spoken of the Roman circus.

**DG:** Another ugly mirror! The same Roman magistrates—the same senatorial elite who calculatingly turned citizens into lynch mobs at gladiatorial games as their most vivid experience of voting—also seem to have invented fanatic team sports with their chariot teams (and "fan," I always remind myself, is just short for "fanatic"). Roman chariot-team fans were famous for regularly rioting, but that was second-order participation. And the "evils of factionalism" were duly added to the list of why democracy would be a terrible system of government—and now, of course, what we call "democracy" is entirely based on the principle of factionalism, which of course it hadn't been before.

So there again the Romans were kind of the evil geniuses here.

The difference between Greek democracy and the modern republican system, which has been redubbed "democracy," are precisely those two inventions: voting over the fate of heroic figures, and factionalism. One came out of gladiators and the other came out of chariot racing.

**MBK:** The circus isn't really participative.

**DG:** No, it isn't. It's precisely how one starts to step away.

**MBK:** The hooligans think they participate but it's an ugly form of virulent spectatorship. If I can recapitulate it simply, for me civil life is based on limiting something that is no longer a predator instinct but a murder drive. Art represents and gives catharsis to this.

**ATZ:** Is there good and bad catharsis, David?

**DG:** I guess the question has to be: is the experience of seeing something horrible on a screen, something that you can't do anything about, modeling the horror... does it ultimately legitimize the horror? Can they throw catharsis back at you and say "The fact that you're taking pleasure in other people's pain means that you're a bad person like everyone else, which is why they deserve the pain"? Can it be used as a way of justifying that?

**MBK:** The question about the function of catharsis should, I think, be dealt with individually per artist.

**ND:** I don't think what David is describing as bad catharsis is really catharsis at all, at least the way I understand it. The concept of catharsis after all comes out of democratic Athens, where, as you point out, tragedy was participatory. The Roman circus is like the horror movie, it isn't actually trying to "purify" anything. Just the opposite.

**DG:** If anything it's meant to make you feel dirty afterwards.

**ND:** When I was studying the history of theatre in Leningrad, my teacher, Vadim Maximov, had a theory of catharsis that was ultimately derived from Vygotsky, and (if I remember it correctly!) was actually very similar to Lacoue-Labarthe's argument that Aristotle's catharsis and Hegel's dialectics are ultimately the same thing. It made a huge impression on me at the time. Maximov argued that true catharsis is always the perfect synthesis of pure form and pure affect. At the point where the two become indistinguishable, that's the moment where you can speak of purification, which is the same as Hegel's absolute, which is by definition beyond morality; you can't speak of "good" or "bad" catharsis.

**DG:** Okay, but then I guess the question is: are there any popular forms that achieve something like catharsis in this participatory sense? (After all, if we're talking about art forms limited only to the rich, it hardly matters, as their very existence is exclusionary.)

All right, how about this: there's a book called *Men, Women, and Chainsaws*, by feminist theorist named Carole Clover where she makes an ingenious interpretation of slasher films. Now, normally slasher movies are considered the lowest of the low when it comes to horror movies, just absolute crap. All slasher movies, she points out, have the same basic structure: you start with point- of-view shots from the perspective of the killer, who kills off a series of (sexualized) women, but then halfway through the movie it switches to the point of view of what's called the "last girl" character, a tomboy, who fights and after many trials and tribulations finally dispatches the murderer. Clover notes that it's easy to sneer at these movies, but you also have to ask who the audience is? Well in this case overwhelmingly teenage boys. That is, people who are moving from a feminized, passive position as children to a masculine, dominant position in society, and are caught uncomfortably between the two. So really the movies are about first killing off the female part of yourself, but then killing off what killed off the female part of yourself, so you achieve a perfect balance. Is that catharsis?

**ND:** Well, I don't know. I've never seen one of those movies.

**DG:** Me neither. They're horrible.

**ND:** But isn't the thing about genres like that, that you watch the same story over and over again? So as catharsis it doesn't really work, in the sense that it doesn't set you free of the problem, Plus it doesn't create any framework for community but just the opposite. If it's preparing you for manhood, what kind of manhood is that? Sitting in a cubicle?

If you're constantly stuck in the same drama that never ends, it's not even tragedy, it's just a gulag. I's not a good piece of art. It's just a bad situation.

## Vampires, cults, hippies

**MBK:** Why are there so many serial killers in America?

**DG:** There are? It's always struck me that America creates a lot more representations of serial killers than it does real ones.

**MBK:** And only of the male ones! When there are a lot of female serial killers too. The difference is just that men only kill unknowns but female serial killers always kill the people they know.

**DG:** I'm not sure that America holds the crown even. I remember once looking up a list of the most prolific serial killers in the world, and I was quite surprised that none of the top ten were American. The biggest country by sheer number of victims seems to be Columbia, with Russia and Brazil piling up some pretty significant body counts too. Of course this also might have something to do with American law enforcement being a bit more competent.

But you're right, serial killers seem to be important to the US sense of itself in some way. It must have something to do with pleonexia, the conception of freedom gone haywire. That is, the idea of a country founded on freedom, but where freedom is ultimately framed in economic terms as the rational realization of ultimately irrational desires—the "pursuit of happiness," as Thomas Jefferson put it.

That's definitely what vampires are all about. At least I've always thought so. Vampires are the ultimate modern monsters. I once read an argument that Dracula is really about the failure of the French Revolution. After all, the revolution was supposed to have killed off all of those bloodsucking aristocrats who live in castles, so as to usher in a domain of equality, fraternity, and enlightened commercial self-interest. There's only one problem. The count refuses to stay dead. He keeps coming back. Why? Well, the implication is obviously that we don't really *want* him to die. We desire him. Because desire is essentially sadomasochistic. All this is true (I mean, the interpretation is true—I don't actually think desire is inherently sadomasochistic), but I'd add another element: the vampire is a figure of control and power. In that way they're the opposite of werewolves: vampires control other creatures, bats and wolves and their hypnotized minions, whereas werewolves can't even control themselves. But ultimately it's all an illusion. Vampires can't control themselves either; they're slaves to the utterly unlimited desire for more and more blood. They grow geometrically, so it doesn't make any sense, just like capitalism doesn't.

**ATZ:** What do you mean, it doesn't make sense?

**DG:** Well, the number of vampires *should* increase geometrically, and since all those vampires have an unlimited need for human blood, eventually everyone would be a vampire. So you have to come up with some reason they don't. Every vampire universe has to solve that logical problem. So you have this fundamentally irrational growth model, which is capitalism.

**MBK:** I'm very impressed.

**DG:** Well, the French Revolution part isn't mine—that was someone named Mark Edmundson—but the rest is. So you could say your mythic serial killer is a secularization of this, in that they're utterly systematic and rational—insofar as they are methodical, and they have to be at least to some extent or else they'd get caught—but they're ultimately based on this unhinged unlimited desire, which they can't stop. Perhaps—I'm just improvising here—if the vampire is really a romanticized figure for capitalism (what's apparently the very opposite of capitalism, the eternal aristocrat, turns out to be just the same thing after all), the serial killer, the modern movie monster who actually does exist, is a figure for the state.

**MBK:** So about anarchism and catharsis and all that we have the beginnings of answer! It's perfectly clear that when you have a smaller society you don't have serial killers. It's the result of maximization.

**DG:** Well, there's also the fact that in a small society a serial killer would be much more likely to get caught. But yes, it's about scale, abstraction, excess.

**ATZ:** How did it start in America?

**DG:** I'm not still not entirely sure it did! Well, do you mean the glorification of serial killers or the appearance of actual serial killers? I guess the first modern serial killer is Jack the Ripper. You don't have anything like that in the US until... what? The Boston

Strangler? Then there was a whole series of other things that happened in the 60s that were unprecedented: the 1966 tower shooting at the University of Texas, for instance. Some ex-marine just climbed up into a tower with a rifle and tried to kill as many people as possible.

**ATZ:** The Sharon Tate case ended the 60s didn't it?

**DG:** Right, right, the cult killing. That was another new one. People said it marked the death of flower power—"Now we see where this hippie stuff really leads." Though of course as we've since learned, that one was very odd. With a few exceptions like Aum Shinriko in Japan, if members of tiny charismatic sects are going to kill anybody, they're just going to kill themselves.

But it's true it entirely destroyed the hippie brand, didn't it? Or something did around that time. I noticed when I was doing my ethnography of direct action that most activists when they're sizing each other up, place each other along a continuum between punk and hippie, but no one *admits* to being a hippie, any more. It's always a bit startling when you see movies from the 60s and people will say "Yes, I'm from the hippie movement!"

The irony is that the Manson Family was actually trying to start a race war—which they assumed would end with black people killing off the non-hippie whites and the Manson family emerging from hiding to rule over them as a new caste of slave-holders. So it's a bit odd to see it as reflecting on counter-cultural rebellion. It's more a story about the core pathology of America itself, a country founded on great crimes (genocide, slavery), which has no substance other than law, but which somehow holds itself out as a light unto nations, a model of redemption. If it can't do that, claim to represent some kind of redemptive future, it seems to just descend into pure nihilism.

I think that's what's been happening. America used to represent the future to the world, though no one was entirely sure what kind of future and how. That didn't matter; the future is inherently mysterious. Now it's caught between a far left trying to establish some kind of social democracy, and a far right trying to create blood-and-soil racialized nationalism. Basically things most countries in the world already had fifty, even a hundred years ago. As a result I think the really significant moments we see here aren't even the emergence of serial killers—who are just secularized vampires—but in the 80s when you first see workplace and school shootings, which have become so commonplace by now that most of them aren't even reported. It's as if America is experiencing some kind of nihilistic insurrection. The massacres just happen every day, and the casualty rate is that of a small civil war. It's just entirely unclear what the sides are.

## Utopia

**ATZ:** Something I would like us to address, which we have been addressing indirectly, is the question of utopia.

**DG:** There you go. [*silence*] Oh, you want me to take that one?

**MBK:** It's a book about David so he'll answer.

**DG:** Oh thanks!

**MBK:** No, but for me utopia is games. We can go from there to the question of politics, which is all about imposing scientific rules. I sometimes think that's the reason Stalinists always say that anarchism leads to fascism; without laws that's all there is. Fascism for them is the speculated ghost of anarchism.

**DG:** Liberals too, unfortunately. Norman Cohn in *The Pursuit of the Millennium* has a famous description of Thomas Muntzer and the Anabaptists, of a movement that starts as a radical anti-authoritarian rebellion degenerates, especially after they are besieged, and turns into total totalitarian power— and it's often presented as a parable for what would necessarily happen to anarchism. If you talk to a Leninist or a Stalinist about anarchism they'll almost invariably try to make the same point by citing an essay by Jo Freeman called "The Tyranny of Structurelessness." Freeman was a feminist organizer in the 70s, when feminist consciousness-raising groups were mostly explicitly anarchist in their organization. But their idea of anarchism was no formal structure, no rules at all. Just improvise in a spirit of sisterhood. The result, she pointed out, was usually that you end up having de facto leadership cliques— some small group of people who will have some affinity: all lesbians, or all not lesbians, or all from wealthy backgrounds, or they all went to the same high school or dropped out of the same male activist group—who end up effectively running everything. The Leninist always cites this to argue that leadership structures are inevitable, so if you don't have a formal one you'll get an informal one based on the control of information and such. So it's better to formalize it, create a steering committee that operates under clear and transparent rules, than an unaccountable informal one. You really wonder what essay these people are reading, or if they've actually read the essay, because that's not what Freeman says at all. She actually ends by saying it's crucial to create clear rules and processes designed to prevent leadership structures from emerging, de facto or otherwise. The whole American anarchist obsession with "process" really traces back to this. In fact the easiest way to tell if you're *not* in an anarchist meeting (and by "anarchist" here I don't necessarily mean capital-A anarchist, but what I'd call small-a anarchist, which follows anarchist principles whatever it may call itself) is whether it's always the same guy leading the meeting, and whether he's making all the proposals. Anarchists are more likely to have an elaborate process of facilitation where there's always two people, usually of mixed gender, facilitating, who never facilitate twice in a row and never bring in proposals themselves.

Then it builds up from there. How do you make sure there's no monopolizing of information? How do you balance the consensus and majority principles? How do you handle the relation of smaller groups and bigger working groups? On the one hand you want to maximize individual bottom-up initiative; on the other hand you want to ensure that everyone gets to weigh in on decisions that effect them. My point is just that there's a long history of anarchist process which is all about solving this problem, and these people ignore that and say "Well the obvious thing to do is to take these inevitable informal cliques and make them official." This is ultimately, I am convinced, an aesthetic impulse. After all, why is it better to have a recognized authoritarian clique with explicit powers than an informal one? The argument is that if the former abuses their power, they can be more easily called out. But a moment's practical reflection makes it clear that this is anything but true. No, actually. They have massive means at their disposal to ensure they're not called out. An informal clique, in contrast, is by definition acting illegitimately and is quite easy to call out. When you push people on this point, they're often willing to admit their objections are ultimately aesthetic, and therefore utopian. It's just kind of unsavory to embrace the idea of unacknowledged powers. Better to at least pretend you have a totally transparent system, even if you know perfectly well that's impossible.

I'm convinced this is one reason anarchism works so well. It doesn't maintain the ideal of perfection that if everyone would just follow the rules, everything will be fine. It assumes a bit of slouching. For instance, kibbutzim or other collectives that operated successfully on directly democratic principles did so because they didn't insist on full attendance. So maybe just a third of membership showed up for most meetings. So what? Some people are process junkies, and actually enjoy meetings. And you could conclude that it's unfair. It means they had the power, but the people who did show up were also operating with the knowledge if they did anything that made anyone angry, that person would definitely start showing up, in the same way as the informal clique was operating with the knowledge that they could be called out at any time.

I actually find it quite ironic that a standard accusation against anarchism is that it has a naïve trust in human nature. But starting at least with Kropotkin, anarchists have always replied "No you are the ones who have a naïve trust in human nature. You think you can make someone a magistrate with the power of life and death over other human beings and he'll always be fair and impartial! That's absurd. You can't just give people arbitrary power over others and expect them not to abuse it."

That's another point I always say about anarchism and human nature. People will insist, "But some people will always be selfish assholes who just care about themselves." Undoubtedly there will still be people who are selfish assholes in the world, even in a stateless society, but at least they won't be in command of armies, which I for one feel is an improvement.

**ND:** So in this way anarchism is if anything anti-utopian?

**DG:** Yes. It is deeply accepting of people as they are.

You could also define anarchy as the absolute rejection of all forms of bullying. One of the most difficult things I ever had to write was a piece on bullying for *The Baffler*—I guess it just struck on very fundamental childhood traumas that I'd largely taught myself not to think about. The ultimate conclusion was that when we look for the critical flaw in human nature, we're probably looking in the wrong places. You'll find a million essays asking why people are mean—why do they have a drive to dominate and humiliate others, why they are bullies—but rarely do you see anyone ask why people who are *not* bullies or sadists make excuses for those who are. Because if you think about it, how many of us are genuine sadists? But even if it's only 1% of the population that even has the potential to be genuinely malicious bullies, it sometimes seems like 97% of the remainder are unwilling to admit it—at least publicly.

I spent some time going through psychological studies of schoolyard bullying, and what I discovered is that most of us are laboring under a whole series of misconceptions on the subject. First, everyone assumes that if you stand up to a bully, you'll just get attacked yourself. Actually that's not true. Bullies tend to rely on the complicity of the audience, but if just a few kids say "Hey, why are you picking on that kid?" or otherwise disapprove, they usually cut it out. Second, bullies don't suffer from low self-esteem. They typically see themselves as totally within their rights enforcing social norms against weakness, effeminacy, incompetence, etc. (and the fact that teachers let them get away with it, that the school prevents the victims from running away, since you can't flee school, implies to them that they are). If they act like self-satisfied little pricks, it's not because they torn by self-doubt but because they actually are self-satisfied little pricks. Finally, what guarantees that someone will be picked on is not necessarily that they're a nerd or a fat girl—or at least, that only comes later—at first it's because they resist ineffectively. If they don't resist at all, bullies will usually leave off; if they hit back effectively, obviously too. But if they make an initial show of resisting then run away, or cry and threaten to call their parents, then they're marked as perfect victim material.

That latter is crucial I think. I still remember in grade school one nasty kid who'd just continually, endlessly jab and attack me every day in ways always calculated to fall just under the radar of the authorities. One day I just couldn't take it any more and knocked him across the hall, and of course, as a result, I was the one who got in trouble. The same pattern though recurs on every level of systematic oppression: class, race, gender. Constant tiny jabs, put-downs, indignities, always calculated to be just at a level where if someone objects, you can pretend it's their indignation that's the issue.

It only works though because the overwhelming majority of onlookers let it happen. The psychological studies show that children who are onlookers tend to dislike both the bully and victim equally. That sounds exactly right. The instinct, on witnessing such things, always seems to be to equate the bully and the victim and try to isolate them in a bubble of reciprocated conflict. You see this on social media all the time; I call it the "you-two-cut-it-out phenomenon." Somebody attacks you, you ignore them. They attack again, you ignore them again. They escalate. You try to rise above. Maybe you even point out what's happening. It doesn't matter. This can happens 25, 35 times and nobody else says a word. Finally, round 36 and you answer back, and instantly half a dozen onlookers jump in to say "Look at those two idiots fighting!" or "Why can't you two just calm down and try to understand the other's point of view" or even insist that your overly exasperated response is far more objectionable than the original 36 unprovoked attacks.

Obviously this is the whole point of trolling, to play on this sort of response. But it's essential to bullying.

You can see the mechanism very clearly in the case of wartime atrocities. If some group starts massacring another, there are so many people whose first reaction will be to search for evidence, any evidence, that will allow them to claim the victims are responsible for some kind of atrocity as well. And if you search hard enough you'll almost invariably turn up something. When I was growing up, we had this friend Harold who had a chicken farm in New Jersey. Harold had been a Jewish partisan in the woods in Poland during the war. At one point, my mother later told me, they'd tried to make contact with the local Polish partisans, but it turns out they were anti-Semites and turned the envoys over to the Nazis. So a week later a few of the Jewish partisans showed up at their town hall during a polka dance and tossed a grenade into the window. Harold didn't know the details of what happened, but innocent people were surely maimed or killed. Was it an atrocity? Sure. Sometimes people in desperate circumstances do atrocious things. Can we then conclude of World War II that "all sides committed atrocities" and leave it at that? That would be insane. But it's exactly the approach most people would be taking if these same events were happening today.

For me the essence of bullying is that it's a form of aggression calculated to provoke a reaction that can then be used as retrospective justification for the initial aggression itself. That's the real core of the thing. I imagine an anarchist social order above all as one where everyone learns to identify this dynamic from childhood, and is inoculated against it.

## Rules of engagement

**DG:** There's a military theorist called Martin Van Creveld who made the same point as Scarry, that Clausewitz's position—that the reason why war is a contest specifically of violence is because a contest of violence is the only one that carries within itself the means of its own enforcement—can't really be true.

Creveld makes the trenchant point that if you look at history, war is anything but an unlimited contest of power; there are always rules. Often very elaborate and intricate ones. There are rules about who is a combatant and who isn't, what you can and can't do with prisoners, messengers, medics, what kinds of weapons and tactics are permissible and what aren't. Even Hitler and Stalin, for instance, agreed never to use poison gas against each other's troops. Part of this is just an extension of the principle of discipline—an army that fights without rules is just a rampaging mob, and when a rampaging mob meets a real army, they always lose. But even more there have to rules because otherwise you don't know who won. Often these rules are very specific: in ancient Greece the battle wasn't over until one side has to ask the other for their dead; in medieval Europe apparently, an army had to stay on the field for three days after the battle so the other side could come back and try again. So the victor was in no sense simply determined by de facto preponderance of force. In fact the only people who systematically broke the rules—Attila the Hun, or Hernán Cortés— tended to be remembered as monsters for centuries after for that very reason.

At the time I read Van Creveld I was involved in the alter-globalization movement and taking part in lots of large-scale direct actions, in Quebec City, Genoa, Washington, New York… It made sense: what I'd been seeing on the streets in many cases exactly resembled ancient warfare, with feints, charges, flanking maneuvers, even helmets and shields. It was just that the rules of engagement were far more limiting. And it suddenly occurred to me, wait a minute, cops break almost all those rules all the time. If you try to negotiate with them, half the time they arrest the go-between. They attack medics all the time. If you declare a "green zone," where no one will do anything illegal, so as to make a safe space for old people or children, the cops will almost invariably teargas or attack it. They act like totally dishonorable opponents.

It's not just that all cops are bastards though. There's a logic. After all, if police were to treat you honorably, that would be recognizing you as an equal party to a conflict. But they represent the state. They're not going to recognize you as the equivalent to the state. That would be recognizing a legitimate dual power situation. That's the last thing cops are going to do. But they can't just kill you, either—especially if you're white.

So the solution: systematically break all the *other* rules.

One corollary of this is that all the most brutal, the most truly vicious wars that have been fought in recent memory are ones which aren't wars at all in the eye of those commanding the largest forces, but police actions. Like Vietnam, or Algeria, or Angola, Syria, Iraq. Not only are they called "police actions," they actually do follow the logic of police, which is to fight a permanent war—the "war on crime"—between the state and an intrinsically dishonorable enemy, one that can never be fully defeated. In part it can't because the "war on crime" itself is a transposition of the underlying war that constitutes the nation to begin with, the permanent war between sovereign and people, which I would argue is prior even to Schmitt's friend/enemy distinction. One could even say the cosmic war that marks the imagination of free societies is brought down to earth. In a way the modern nation-state is just a truce, a "social peace" established between two warring parties, sovereign and people. It's transposed onto a "war on crime," and then of course the "war on drugs" (the first to go international) and "war on terror." All of them are permanent wars against an inherently dishonorable opponent that cannot, however, be defeated. Because it's not like crime, or drugs, or terror, are going to surrender and cease hostilities.

Something most people don't remember is that at the very beginning of the guerrilla war in Iraq, one of the rebel groups captured an American soldier. They announced "Okay, we got one of your guys. We will observe the Geneva conventions on prisoners of war; we will treat them according to the law and expect you to treat our prisoners the same. We would be interested in organizing some kind of exchange." And the Americans immediately responded "What? No! We don't negotiate with terrorists." So the Iraqi guerrillas said "Okay fine. Have it your way. We'll kill him."

And people wonder how Daesh happened. The first impulse of the Iraqi resistance was to say "Let us engage in honorable combat." And the response was "Absolutely not. This isn't a war, it's a police action. You're inherently dishonorable in our eyes and therefore we have no intention of observing anything like the Geneva convention. Negotiations and law are for people we respect, like the crazed Salafi Kingdom of Saudi Arabia."

Things like this kept happening. Eventually those resisting imperial power figure out that they're only taken seriously if they cast themselves in a certain role, as the villain in a Christian drama—so they start playing along. If you look at the early videos of ISIS, with their parades of black flags, sinister hooded figures, beheadings and crucifixions and burnings at the stake, it's as if they'd gone through every movie they could find to get a sense of what the ultimate Middle Eastern Bond villain would be like and tried to see if they could do it one better.

I think the War on Terror was an attempt to solve a problem. It didn't work. But the problem was the same one I described briefly before: the pieces of the nation-state, which we're used to thinking just somehow naturally go together, are in the process of drifting apart. So we have the emergence of a global administrative bureaucracy, but without the other two components: neither a principle of sovereignty, nor a heroic field of political contention. Since World War II the US has been constructing the world's first planetary administrative system. Starting with the Bretton Woods institutions (the IMF, World Bank, World Trade Organization—which incidentally are all formally part of the UN), but including private and public elements ranging from treaty organizations like the EU or NAFTA, to transnationals NGOs, even credit rating institutions. The alter-globalization movement was an attempt to expose and challenge that system—until Seattle or A16, most people in the US didn't even know the WTO or IMF even existed. It was remarkably effective. Within a very short period of time, the IMF had effectively been kicked out of the vast majority of the world's countries; social movements were coordinating everywhere; after Seattle every single attempt to negotiate a trade treaty collapsed and failed.

Obviously this is not the way they teach us history, because in official histories social movements are insignificant. But all of us who were there at the time were aware the ruling class was in a minor panic. Then 911 happens and they declare war. But of course the War on Terror wasn't a war at all; it was an attempt to create a logic of police on a planetary level, the kind of war you know you'll never win. The "forever wars," some people started calling them. In other words, to create a single principle of sovereignty to back up the global administrative structure. But that clearly didn't work.

It surprises me how weak most of the theorizing on such matters is. Perhaps it's yet another example of people insisting on using very pure, rarified versions of reality in abstract discussion, however complicated and messy the reality—like the way everyone pretended there were states in the Middle Ages, even though no one actually lived in one. Every time we talk about "war" in the abstract, we imagine two states—they each have an army, they declare war on each other, and they fight it out until one side surrenders, or there's some kind of peace treaty... Since World War II has there been a single war that actually took that form? The Arab-Israeli conflict?

**ND:** No!

**ATZ:** Neither side even recognizes the enemy's sovereignty.

**ND:** Yes, from the Arab side too in the beginning it was a police operation. And at this point no one even seems to want to end it, there are too many interests invested in its prolongation.

**DG:** So I guess it really was World War II!

Even when Saddam Hussein invades Kuwait he has to make up an imaginary Kuwaiti rebel organization that he's coming to assist. We all operate with an abstract idea of what a war is like, even though we're keenly aware that virtually no war actually takes that form.

**ND:** That's why there are no rules, no victory, and no catharsis.

**ATZ:** I think we can find something by thinking about the bullying you-two-cut-it-out phenomenon and the we-don't-negotiate-with-terrorists phenomenon.

**DG:** Ah, very interesting. Please do go on.

**ATZ:** One is to negate the enemy, saying that they're beyond reasoning ("We don't negotiate with terrorists"), and the other to insist on enmity, equating the victim and the bully just by virtue of them being put in dialectic by the attack.

And I think it has to do with the idea of dignity, and the moral attribution by a third party, which is the spectator... let's see where my mind wants to go...

I think there's a parallel between the spectator with the power to decide who is an honorable opponent and the relativistic cop from earlier.

**DG:** Yes, that makes a lot of sense.

Let's figure this out.

Okay, I definitely agree the spectator in the bullying scenario is crucial. One of the points I made in the original piece was that psychologists find that in schoolyard bullying other kids don't like the bully very much, but they feel that they shouldn't intervene because it would just make things worst, or alternately because they'd get bullied too. They also find that that isn't true: if one or two kids object, they'll usually stop. So why is that everybody has this idea in their head about what would happen if you stepped up? Where does it come from?

Part of the reason is popular culture (that's what the superhero genre is about, to tell you that if you say "Hey why are you beating up on that kid?" then you'd better be prepared to take on a creature from outer space that can shoot death-rays from its eyes). But even more because in adult life that does happen—in the workplace, bullies tend to be scrupulously protected, as I discovered to my chagrin at Yale. And if you tell a cop "Hey why are you beating up on that kid? He didn't do anything," you may well end up in serious trouble. In fact the civilians most likely to end up seriously injured by police turn out to be precisely such good Samaritans.

It struck me that *this* is the real primordial scene of power. Not the Hegelian master-slave dialectic, which for some reason has gotten lodged in the literature as the deep structure of power—because seriously, how often do we really witness two people engaged in a life- and-death struggle for recognition? Basically never. On the other hand, all of us have witnessed, and played one or another role in, scenes where one person is pummeling another and both of them are appealing to some third party or parties for recognition. The victim calls out for sympathy; the aggressor tries to represent the victim's reaction as retrospective pretext for their initial aggression. That trinary bullying scene is the real structure of power. That's the real thing.

**ATZ:** So the onlooker is simultaneously the most powerful actor and the most passive one? On the one hand they hold the power of representation, siding with the one or the other narrative. This agency is only increased by their position of "once removed" from the scene. Yet that is also what condemns them to a form of passivity in assessment.

**DG:** You're basically challenging me to put all these pieces together, aren't you? It's true that sometimes I resist doing that; I'm not sure why. I guess I'm afraid of creating anything that might be turned into a totalizing system. But if I were to give it a shot…

You plug these various scenarios into this trinary structure, so what do you get? Officer Mindfuck, the relativist cop, is basically the same as the cop who's beating up the good Samaritan for trying to intervene. Because he insists there are no higher criteria which could possibly justify intervention. I once read a former policeman turned sociologist make the point that cops almost never beat up burglars, because burglars are playing the same game as the cops are: law and order. Real violence only comes in when someone "talks back," that is, challenges their "right to define the situation" by insisting there's another game; who says "Wait a minute, this isn't a possible crime situation, it's a citizen-who-pays-your-salary-walking-his-dog   situation," or "This isn't a disorderly crowd, it's an expression of freedom of assembly," etc. That's when the stick comes out.

This is incidentally where the giant puppets come in. A mass direct action like at the 1999 WTO meetings at Seattle or the 2001 Summit of the Americas in Quebec City was an attempt to create an "event," or a moment of revolutionary creativity. That both meant taking what seemed absolute, permanent, and monumental and making them seem brittle and ephemeral and vulnerable, and it also meant taking things that seemed brittle and ephemeral, and showing that they could quite easily become absolute and monumental. One of the things that fascinated me about the symbolism of the global-justice movement—which real established the mythological language that was then taken up in Occupy and subsequent movements—was that... well, if you asked the average American about Seattle, or later summit mobilizations, the two things they were likely to know were, first, that there were masked anarchists dressed in black smashing Starbucks' windows, and second, that there colorful giant puppets. The thing that fascinated me was why was it the cops always seemed to hate the puppets more?

Well, the symbolism was easy enough to read. The Black Bloc collective at Seattle was quite explicit about what they were doing. They even issued a manifesto saying "We are surrounded by neon and glass, this glittering fantasy world of consumer capitalism, and we think of it as permanent and monumental, but all you have to do is get a hammer and the whole thing dissolves away." As Bakunin put it, "The urge to destroy is also a creative urge." We need to remind people that these things aren't really ineffable. But the puppets, the carnival bloc surrounding them with the clowns and belly dancers and klezmer bands and fairies with feather dusters tickling the police and whatnot... that was the other side of the same equation. Puppets were gigantic papier-mâché gods and dragons and demons and effigies but they were also obvious ridiculous, a mockery of the very idea of a monument. They are monuments one can improvise overnight in a big party and then set on fire afterwards. They allude to the permanent potential to create new verities, new social forms, and then toss them away again if necessary. So in that sense they have to be kept ridiculous, because otherwise they'd be utterly terrifying.

Another way to put this of course is that they represented the play principle in its purest form. And of course gods at play are by definition terrifying. Not only was it what they represented; it's also how they were actually deployed—the puppets and surrounding carnival bloc were, typically, sent in to defuse situations of potential conflict, particularly where the police seemed likely to attack. They were an attempt to change the rules of the game when those rules seemed like they were likely to lead to violence. But from the perspective of the cops, I think, that was totally cheating. You're supposed to negotiate the rules of engagement indirectly, through the law and media. Anarchists were trying to renegotiate the rules on the field of battle itself. So of course the cops would just go completely berserk and try to destroy the puppets. It got so that we had to start making the puppets in secret, because if the police got wind of where the warehouses were, they'd sweep in and try to take them out in a preemptive strike.

**ATZ:** Now, what about the War on Terror?

**DG:** I guess it makes sense that the War on Terror was the response. It was an attempt to permanently redefine the rules of engagement. The alter-globalization movement had been astonishingly successful—

people forget that now—but of course wiping out such feelings of possibility, making them seem unreal, foolish, is precisely what the game of power is ultimately all about. But it's true: within just a few years we destroyed an almost total ideological hegemony, kicked the IMF out of most of the world and brought it to the brink of bankruptcy, put the question of global democracy on the table (as in: what would that even mean?). We were all startled how quickly it happened. So the response was a direct attack on the political imagination.

In practice, you could say it's all about who gets to negotiate the rules of engagement and who is equal parties to it. "Terrorists" by definition don't, and aren't. The you-two-cut-it-out fallacy is basically a refusal, on the part of the audience, to relegate the aggressor to the status of terrorist (or bully—here it's essentially the same thing). You're saying "No, as far as I'm concerned you're both moral equivalents here."

**ATZ:** Oh! Okay. I think I get it. Well, I get something. So the argument is just about having the means to always insist that you are David and the other person is Goliath no matter what. In the same way that we say "We don't negotiate with terrorists," we tell kids who are bullied to not try and reason with the bullies. By refusing to negotiate with Al Qaeda or whoever else, you keep the victimhood pure.

**DG:** Do we tell them that? Well, I guess *if* we recognize it as true bullying.

This is where the weird insistence you see all the time in the literature in the 60s—for example, that school bullies must have been victimized them-selves, they must be cowering insecure victims deep inside—is really telling. Let me make a confession here. I'm hesitant to tell the story, because it's about my father...

Now, my dad was a leftist hero of a sort. He'd vol-unteered to fight in the International Brigades; in many ways he was really an anarchist. But towards the end of his life he was very bitter, and one way it manifested itself was he developed a few odd right-wing attitudes: he'd get drunk and rant at the TV, mainly, about "liberal judges" who let off violent criminals on technicalities or gave them slap-on-the-wrist sentences because of their disadvantaged backgrounds. I could never figure out why. Sure it was New York in the 70s. It was a rough town, but he was never a crime victim and never lived in a dangerous neighborhood. Only much later I real-ized it was all about me and my brother. We'd been bullied in school, mainly by other working class kids for being bookish, and I later learned he'd tried to intervene with the school authorities repeatedly, and they'd lectured him about how the bullies came from disadvantaged backgrounds and were just act-ing out (he also knew how I had been punished for fighting back). So of course he felt entirely emas-culated; he couldn't protect his own children. But now that I think of it, he took exactly the same atti-tude to terrorists, another of his pet peeves. When I would ask "Well, what do you think the terrorists are thinking, what are they trying to achieve?" he became furious and basically told me it was wrong to even speculate.

But of course as it turns out bullies mostly aren't insecure victims themselves. In fact some of the ones I still remember were from much wealthier families—I think one now is a TV news executive or somesuch.

If you think about it—I mean, I haven't really, but I am now—terrorism is just the bullying of the weak, just as bullying is the terrorism of the strong. In each case it's an attempt to provoke a response that you can then blame the target for. This is true even in the most subtle, conversational forms:

"You're a decent chap, Jeeves, but your mother really failed to teach you manners."

"Wait, why are you bringing my mother into this? Stop being an asshole."

"See what I mean? He called me an asshole! You heard that didn't you, everyone? Asshole! He called me an asshole!"

Terrorism is actually an attempt to do the same. Usually you're trying to provoke a government to repress a certain group of people—precisely those whom you claim to represent—so as to mobilize them politically. Say I'm a Ruthenian separatist in some imaginary country. So what's my biggest problem? Likely as not that members of the Ruthenian minority either don't want their own separate state, or don't care enough to do much about it. But if I put a few bombs in marketplaces and loudly declare it was the Ruthenian liberation movement that did it, well, chances are the government, and particularly the security forces, will start making the lives of Ruthenians very unpleasant. It's an attempt to provoke what you believe to be a repressive state to act even more repressively.

But isn't that just ultimately the same logic of bullying? An unprovoked attack designed to provoke a response that can become its own retrospective justification. Only in this case it becomes a way of reversing the logic of bullying back on those in the dominant position.

**ATZ:** Absolutely. Something is there. And it goes back and forth because the terrorists are the product of bullying in the first place.

**DG:** Yes! Maybe not in the case of schoolchildren, but definitely in the case of terrorists. Well, there have been one or two extremely cynical exceptions: South African intelligence once created an insurgency in Mozambique basically by finding a few kids from ethnic minorities, paying them large amounts of money to put bombs in marketplaces in the name of imaginary separatist groups, and essentially creating real separatist groups by so doing. But that's obviously unusual.

When it comes to Israeli policy on the West Bank, for example, well the thing that really struck me when I went there was the Israeli occupations was clearly designed to make everyone's life unliveable in a thousand different ways, but any given one of them was so minor it wouldn't seem to justify a violent response. So it was just like that kid in gym class constantly kicking and jabbing you. Or like the North Korean tactic of interrogating foreign prisoners by making them sit on the edge of a chair for eight hours, or lean against a wall in an uncomfortable way—after a while, it's just impossible, but try going to the International Tribunal on Torture and telling them you've been made to sit on the edge of a chair for a really long time.

So when some Palestinian actually does finally lash out it seems entirely disproportionate, and the Israelis can say "Aha! Look at them, they're just a bunch of terrorists." But then the logic on the other side becomes "Well as long as some people are going to be lashing out anyway, let's do it in a systematic way."

But in that case the Israeli side has managed to almost entirely win the battle over the terms of engagement. They can open fire on twelve-year-olds with rocks or even just kids standing nearby one with total impunity.

**ATZ:** So how could you actually change that?

**DG:** Well, first of all, I think Palestinians and their supporters have to reengage on the level of myth. There was an action some years ago where Palestinian activists resisting a farm eviction painted themselves blue and dressed up like the Na'vi in *Avatar* and hugged trees. And of course the IDF opened fire on them anyway. I thought that was absolutely brilliant. But it'll take enormous amounts of work to start replacing existing images in the heads of, say, Americans with ones like that.

# Dual sovereignty

**ATZ:** Right, so in all of these cases there's a shared logic to the ways in which cops deny sovereignty.

**DG:** Yes, since they embody the sovereignty of the state, they can't by definition treat you as an equal.

**ATZ:** So then the whole issue is with the concept of zero sum sovereignty.

**DG:** Yeah, exactly. That's why my first step to understand how we get to an anarchic state of affairs, how a revolution could work today, necessarily passes through some idea of dual sovereignty.

**ND:** Dual sovereignty?

**DG:** Because we're not going to have an insurrectionary moment where the state just falls away. That's one reason I'm so interested in Rojava, which is in a way historically unique, because the same people created what are essentially both sides of a dual power situation. In Northeast Syria right now (hopefully still when this goes to publication, since inevitably they've been labeled "terrorists" and are under genocidal attack), have both a top-down and a bottom-up structure. The first is they can deal with the international community and people who expect there to be something that looks like a state, with ministers, a parliament, and so on; and the bottom-up as a form of constituent direct democracy, based on nested assemblies which start with just a few hundred people. They insist it's not a state, though, because anybody with a gun is answerable to the bottom-up groups rather than the top-down ones. The top-down ones are just there for administrative purposes, guidance, negotiating with outsiders… rather like an Amazonian chief, in fact.

One reason that even as an anarchist I get along with a lot of the Labour left in the UK is that they understand this. They actually say "We don't want to co-opt the extra-parliamentary left. We want to have you out there on the streets doing things more radical than we can, so as to create a synergy which will drive the general direction of society to the left." I've heard John McDonnell say this frequently: the only way social progress has ever happened in the UK is by a judicious combination of "parliamentary action, radical trade unionism, and insurrection—or, as they more politely like to put it nowadays, 'direct action'." (That's an actual quote.) What's more, they seem to be genuinely sincere about it. They want to figure out how the parliamentary and extra-parliamentary left can find a synergy rather than undercut each other. Then of course you have movements like the Gilets Jaunes creating an entirely new dimension of politics within the society, antagonistic to traditional forms of power.

# Against the politics of opinion

**DG:** It's the absence of those kinds of dual power structures which leaves us mired in the politics of opinion.

Some years ago, when I was writing about education, I came on the idea of writing a systematic critique of the very notion of "opinion." What is an "opinion" anyway? Opinions are things you have when you don't have any power. After all, presidents don't have opinions. Prime ministers don't have opinions. They have policies. That's why opinions often take on this free floating quality, unmoored to practical considerations. "Oh, I say we just lock them all up." "Let's just pull out of the UN, then," and so forth. You could say it's another variation on the ugly-mirror phenomena. If you make it clear to people that what they say makes no difference anyway, well, a lot of them are likely to say really irresponsible things and that'll just reinforce the impression that it would be a bad idea to give them any say in important decisions. But in a way this extremism is itself a protest against the fact that what they say doesn't matter, because if you put those same people in a process of real deliberation, they'll behave entirely differently.

**ATZ:** What about Brexit?

**DG:** Case in point. Brexit is a perfect example of how *not* to make decisions; there was no deliberative process, just a sounding of opinions. (This is even aside from the point that as anyone who does direct democracy knows, 52–48 is a tie. If that's your result, you asked the question wrong and need to do it again.) It's a way of teaching people "See what happens when you act out of your opinion? Shut up and let us run things."

Ultimately I think it's a product of our education system, where children are constantly asked their views even though they know no one actually cares and their views makes no difference. I'm thinking here of the American system particularly.

**ATZ:** What sorts of opinions are they asked for?

**DG:** All sorts. It doesn't matter. In Europe if you write a paper, you usually defend one of two or three possible positions. In the US you can say anything you want. It all traces back to Thomas Dewey, who wanted to democratize the American education system. It was very well meaning, so kids are always being asked "Well what do you think about this? What do you think about that?"

**ND:** That's the liberal arts tradition, which is a very elitist one.

**DG:** Yes, and ultimately as I say an illusion. It would be very different if children occasionally got to make actual decisions that effected them in some way.

**ATZ:** But it's true that even outside of the education system we're constantly asking [*condescending voice*] "Did you like that?" And what, if they say no? Are we going to do anything about it?

**DG:** Exactly! And all this effects how people communicate. They have no experience of deliberation, of mutual listening, exploring one another's perspectives, aside from very immediate practical problem-solving perhaps. If you talk about how to fix the stove, maybe, they can engage. But beyond that, well, I've noticed that, at least with those who haven't gone through the higher education system, the instinct is just to exchange opinions, so you feel like you're playing some kind of ping-pong.

My mother was an extremely intelligent person, already in college at age 16, though after a year she had to drop out to get a factory job to help support the family. It used to frustrate me sometimes, talking to her, because she'd always play ping-pong. That's what it's like with so many opinions: you give your opinion, they give theirs, then maybe you give another of your own… You never really engage. So for a while I thought, well, maybe higher education isn't as useless as I thought. The one thing that people do seem to learn, at least, is to argue at least a little like philosophers, to say "Okay, if you're saying that, would that also mean this?" They're capable of exploring the integrity of another person's ideas.

But then I realized, wait, that's not true. Because children do that all the time. In fact it sometimes seems that's all kids do. "Okay, but if you are saying that, why don't you also say this or that." "But if that's true," and so on interminably sometimes. So the real truth of the education system is that at first we beat that instinct out of them, and then, only later, put it halfway back in for a select elite.

So what would education be like if it didn't do that?

**ND:** In Jewish education there's the built-in reproduction of culture, very complex mechanisms of
how family are arranged and kids are taught.

**DG:** I guess the question would be how to begin with
some form of deliberation rather than opinion-mak-
ing as a model for how to think.

**MBK:** For me that's the idea of the game of politics as
the research of rules. Opinions are attempts to construct a big entity, which often is called God, which
is really the perfect game.

**DG:** God is the perfect game?

**MBK:** Yes. And a judgment is always an approxima-
tion of what would be perfect politics. I think we're
far from it, but that's my pessimism.

**ATZ:** That's really interesting, if we come back to
the process of follow-through thought that David
just spoke about. This form of reasoning is only halfway reintroduced in university because we learn to
apply it only with malice or bad will. You use follow-through logic to tie your opponents hands: "If
you believe this, do you also believe that?" trying to
disprove the integrity of their thought. It becomes a
rhetorical thing. That's definitely an issue with the
expectation of total coherence that again is an inex-
act representation. Whereas with children, mostly
anyway, are just trying to scout out the landscape of
your statement, accepting the strangest topologies
as long as the speaker is committed to them.

**ND:** And when you don't have access to the framework, the rules of the game, you bring in violence.

## The world upside down (and the mind always upward)

**ATZ:** What I'm hoping we may be able to do throughout the conversation is to try and see that perhaps there is—it would be lovely if there was—some kind of systematic inversion of these things.

**DG:** Of which things?

**ATZ:** You know, my ramble earlier. The real and the unreal, anarchist politics and conventional politics, ugly mirror of society, and unlimited care/freedom, power and counterpower... I'm just hoping to see whether or not there's something slightly systematic in the relation that these inversions have with each other.

And maybe that's the issue with the value system we're in now, which is so consciously crafted to appear to be no such thing, taking "infravalues" as "metavalues."

**DG:** Oh no... I had been trying to avoid value theory!

**ATZ:** I'd like us to go back and see what we come up with around the question of "operating at a different level of emergence than the one you speak on."

**DG:** Ah, you're referring to Vygotsky's notion of the proximal level of development!

**ATZ:** Guess so. And so the link between that: the fact that we're always operating at a level superior to what we can articulate. And perhaps things we've circled around: the shift of representation from practice.

**DG:** Right, because it points in two different directions. Isn't that interesting? There must be something going on there for us to figure out. If we cracked that one, we'd get the secret of history. [*laughter*]

We can do it! We're almost there!

Ok so, let's give it a go. I'm going to apologize to Mehdi here—what Assia is basically asking is that I see how this fits with a theoretical framework I developed in my work on value theory, which is in its own way very idiosyncratic and arcane. It's my version of an approach developed by one of my anthropological mentors, Terry Turner, who was a Piagetian Marxist (perhaps the only one, come to think of it, unless you want to count Piaget himself). Turner argued that when Marx talks about fetishism, he's really talking about the coordination of multiple perspectives on a complex totality. If the totality is too complex, it just becomes impossible.

In this sense, Marx's fetishism is just a social version of Piagetian egocentrism. I assume you're familiar with the basic concept: children literally see themselves as the center of the universe; they mistake their own perspective on things with the objective nature of reality, which is why, for instance, you can't play hide-and-go-seek with a very small child, because as soon as you vanish, they forget that you ever existed. And it takes a surprisingly long time before children understand the reversibility of relations. For instance, the fact that if I have a brother named Jacques, then Jacques also has a brother, who is me.

Children eventually figure this out but in social relations there's too much going on, and anyway some parts of the picture are made intentionally invisible, like who actually designs and makes those things you use every day. So you end up confusing your own particular vantage on a totality with the nature of the totality itself. Because from the consumer's perspective, commodity fetishism is true: toothbrushes do just jump out of the store all keen to brush your teeth, etc. From the perspective of a bond trader, money does flee markets and pork bellies really do do this and that...

I would add that "fetishism" is a curious expression, because it implies a kind of awareness that something isn't real. The term was originally applied by European merchants and adventurers to African objects that were often used to seal agreements, basically, to create new social relations—for instance, trade pacts with visiting foreigners such as themselves—often, by choosing some completely random but striking-looking object and declaring it a god capable of enforcing the terms of the contract. Those who did insisted they believed these objects were gods, but they didn't really act as if they believed it, since gods could be created or cast away at will. Capitalist fetishists are precisely the opposite: if you point out to a commodities trader talking about how gold is doing this, or pork-bellies doing

that, that gold or pork bellies don't really "do" anything, they'll look at you like you're an idiot—obviously it's just a figure of speech. But really it isn't.
They just assume of course they really don't believe
it, but in fact they do, since they act as if they do.

At any rate, the idea is that commodity fetishism, the fetishism of money or what-have-you, is a
perfectly accurate descriptions of reality from the
fetishist's own situated perspective, but the problem
is the fetishist is confusing his positionality with the
totality. This does assume there *is* a totality, which
is of course precisely the point of attack that post-
structuralists take—but that's a very long argument
and best not got into it here. I will say this: in the
case of creating new social relations, as the African
merchants were doing when they "made a fetish" to
create a trade deal, or say the Six Nations did when
they used wampum to create a confederation, well
then, you could argue, there is no totality yet. The
totality is created through the very act of invoking
it, so at moments like that, you could say, fetishism
*could* be true, or at least half true. In fact I've sometimes defined politics itself in these terms: where
you can make things true just by convincing people
that they are true. If I can convince everyone in the
world I can fly and I jump off a cliff, I'm still dead. If
I convince everyone in the world I'm the Pope, then
I'm the Pope. That's really all there is to it. That's
why the domain of politics always seems to hover
halfway between poetry and just outright fraud.

This is the point where Turner brings in Vygotsky.
Vygotsky is mainly famous for figuring out that
people are always operating on one level of complexity higher than they can actually articulate.

You can speak grammatically before you can actually explain the rules of grammar to anyone, or even understand them if they're explained to you. Actually, for Vygotsky, even thought is just internalized speech: you start by talking, then internalize it. But critically, once you can understand the logic of own actions, say, once you grasp the rules of grammar, by doing so, you're necessarily creating another level of complexity beyond that, which of course you can't completely understand. And so on ad infinitum.

Now it's obvious why this sort of thing would be of interest to anthropologists: this is what we do, to tease out the underlying logic of forms of action that the actors themselves can't fully articulate or even understand. But Turner's real breakthrough—well, he thought it was a breakthrough, and I'm inclined to agree—was to say "Aha! This is why you have myth and ritual."

Take Van Gennep's famous notion of the liminal stage in ritual. This is very Anthro 101, but it's a useful illustration. Say you have a rite of passage, a bunch of girls are initiated into adulthood and become women. If you pass between two categories of being, from girl to a woman, or living to dead, or whatever, there's always a "liminal" stage in between where you're neither, and in that phase all sorts of strange things happen. Social relations are either put on hold or take weird distorted forms; people act like things and things like people; everyone pretends they're a ghost or animal, and so forth. Well, what's really happening here, he suggests, is that by asserting that "girl" and "woman" are equivalent terms, you are necessarily creating a higher level of structure which allows passage between them, which is necessarily incomprehensible from that level. So it seems like some bizarre topsy-turvy Never Never land. Any time you do something twice and say it's the same thing, by that action you're creating a higher level of structure in the Vygotskian sense. If you arrange a marriage, sure, you can see that particular marriage as something you created yourself, jointly with others. But by doing so you're also part of a larger process of reproducing the phenomena of "marriage" itself, and that's the level that's much harder to get your head around. So people will say ""our marriage was arranged by our parents, but the institution of marriage was given to us at the beginning of time by a giant bird," or somesuch.

Essentially, for Turner, all myth and ritual is Vygotsky's proximal level of development on a social level.

What you're trying to figure out now is that we've got two problems that seem complementary but opposite. One is the Vygotskian idea that we're always operating on one level of complexity higher than what we can articulate and represent. The other is the way that representations so often precede the reality. In that the representation of the state precedes the actual creation of the state, the representation of the maximizing economic individual (largely) precedes maximizing economic behavior, and so on ... So how do we reconcile those two?

It seems that they are both equally true. When a medieval writer talks about the state as though there is one, it's not simply a misunderstanding. Rather than talking about feudalism and the reality of parcelized sovereignty, of different types of power interacting in complex ways, they write that this is a very simplified version of a state which would come about three hundred years later. Similarly, when they talk about property they talk about individual property, even though feudal property was endlessly complex. And again, when they talk about individual motivation they talk about this Augustinian pleonetic maximizing of individuals, even though no one acted that way.

My initial guess would be that these schematic, simplified versions stand in for the unfathomable complexities of the proximal level. At first they're just shorthand. But as soon as they enter into political struggle, they're easily adopted as weapons.

**MBK:** That's what I was saying yesterday about language missing its goal and creating a reality more complex than language. For me the movement you describe is that at first there's a representation, then there's a hypostasis, and you give the representation more importance than the phenomena leading it. For me anarchy in the philosophical sense of the term is to deconstruct that hypostasis.

**DG:** Yes, since that hypostasis is the very essence of authority.

## God as transgression and anarchy as God

**DG:** For the Dinka, before they make a sacrifice everyone has to confess their wrongdoings and at least temporarily resolve their problems and difficulties with one another before they can kill the animal and distribute the meat. (In much the same way as Aztec warriors, just before they went into battle together, would have to confess who'd been sleeping with each other's wives.) And the moment of that communion, when they are all eating together having forgiven each other, is God.

There has to be an act of transgression—murder, even—but the result of that act of transgression is the creation of God as a form of utopia.

**MBK:** I think that the strong idea in Judaism is of a God that doesn't exist yet.

People hate Jews because there is this idea of a God that doesn't exist yet. It's a very complicated and frustrating idea. For me, in Judaism there is an assumption of frustration.

Religious socialists and anarchists each demanded the kingdom of God to be realized in this world, and they turned for this purpose to teachings of prophets, that the sole and absolute law of God excludes any other claims to absoluteness. Not only by the representatives of God but also by the state.

**ATZ:** The history of Jewish anarchism or/and Yiddish anarchism is very interesting. You know, you have the very central place of the question—and deliberation as we spoke earlier—that gives Jewish education a huge regenerative potential. Then of course it isn't unified under any high authority, no equivalent to the Pope or the Grand Mufti. Rabbis are simply people with a lot of studying behind them, and at least for the secular representatives at a national level they are elected.

What is great is that this lack of ideological consensus and authority coexists with deep unity in Jewishness that is something of a mystery. Perhaps it has something to do with the community of purpose and irreconcilable perspective on things that we spoke of. Jewish law doesn't contain a "belief" clause at all. This allows for a diversity of internal lives. And then there's the fact that the theological tradition is dialogic, of course, and the Talmud is studied as a trans-historical debate. So that negotiating rules with each other—and with God—is the most important part of the game.

**ND:** There's a joke about a Jew who finds himself stranded on an island. When they come to rescue him, after a few years, they find he's not only built a synagogue, he's built two. So they ask him why he should need two different synagogues when he's only one person, and he answers "Well this one is the synagogue I go to, and this one is the synagogue I would never go to!" So there is always this kind of internal conflict and the reproduction of culture is totally dialogical.

**ATZ:** The Israeli government was struggling recently with the ultra-orthodox community, who were exempt from army service for a while. Now it's being decided that they should serve like everyone else, but the Haredim refuse, so sometimes they get locked up. But when they do they just keep on discussing the Torah in jail, and that's all it takes for it to turn into a Yeshiva. So unless you put everyone in solitary confinement...

**DG:** ... which presumably they would do if they were Arabs, but they aren't.

**ATZ:** Precisely. So there's something about the absolute fluidity of that organization around the dialectic that's a cause for resilience. But that's a tangent.

**DG:** Yeah, I wasn't going to say anything, but now the book, when we do write it up, is going to have some section that says "Chapter 8: Jews."

**MBK:** Even if not, for me it's very interesting, because I didn't dare ask the question of Judaism and anarchy.

**DG:** Come to think of it, I guess you're the only person here who isn't Jewish.

Perhaps we can say that the whole point of anarchism is to create God in the Dinka sense. Or perhaps gods in the fetish sense: to make promises and thus improvise the divine.

**ATZ:** A commitment to the kingdom of God on earth.

**MBK:** Jean-Luc Nancy says that Judaism is atheism plus God.

**DG:** Brilliant. So is God the ultimate event?

**MBK:** Probably!

**ND:** I want to return to the joke about the Jew building the two synagogues because Judaism is so plural. You have the equivalent Israeli joke that if you have two Israelis in a room you'll have five political parties.

**DG:** Not just Israelis! In Madagascar they say that if you have five Malagasy in a room you have eight political parties.

**ND:** But it's not just that they're fractious. What the story of the synagogue suggests, to me at least, is that the fractiousness *is* their unity. Someone said that since the destruction of the Temple, when *we* stopped offering animals in sacrifice, the only unity Jews had were rules about how to argue about the rules.

**ATZ:** [*laughs*] So then the thread is an inherent anarchy in the organization which leads to a proliferation of so many different forms of spirituality and theology but with a defining feature which is…

**DG:** Questioning.
I think.
It sounds anyway like you're suggesting that insofar as Judaism is an attempt to create God, it's an attempt to create God *through* argument. One doesn't air all one's quarrels so as to be pure, and thus capable of approaching the divine; it's the airing the quarrels that is the divine, which one then celebrates.
Well, I started with dialogue, and why dialogue is the model for thought, and I keep getting back to that. We've created this idea that we start as isolated self-conscious individuals and only then enter dialogue. Instead of dialogue being, as Vygotsky or

Bakhtin would have it, the starting point that makes reflective thought possible, we flip it around and treat individual consciousness as the starting point, so that you can have philosophers trying to solve the "other minds" problem (how to prove anyone else even exists), as if the very French or English or German language in which the words "other minds problem" is written was something they had themselves invented and then somehow forgot they'd invented it.

Maybe at this point I'm able to add something to that. When I was writing about "baseline communism," the fact that all human sociality is premised on a certain minimal assumption of "from each according to their abilities, to each according to their needs," well, one obvious case seemed to be language. Conversation is presumed to be cooperative unless there's some reason for it not to be. It never occurs to you that a stranger will give you wrong directions, even though he has no particular reason to give you the right ones. Obviously there are a thousand ways to be cruel using words, but when you really want to express antipathy to someone, you stop speaking to them entirely. Why's that? Presumably, because any verbal interaction would normally imply a responsibility to your interlocutor that you don't want to acknowledge. A certain baseline communism.

Any form of communism, in turn, throws up a shadow of eternity. If direct action is (as I've sometimes argued) the defiant insistence on acting as if one is already free (even though you know you really aren't), then communism is the defiant insistence on acting as if one's friends, family, neighborhood, society, will be around forever (even though one knows they really won't). Though when speaking of baseline communism, of society at large, well, yes, in a sense it's is true. You don't have to keep track of who owes what to whom because there will always be people to give us a light, or directions, or save us when we're drowning.

So within that dialogic basis for all thought there's already the shadow of a communistic eternity, of the Dinka God. But to realize itself it has to pass through conflict, argument, or it's meaningless, infantile, ultimately false. Love without at least some tiny element of hatred is just stupidity. The whole apparatus we've been trying to develop, however embryonically, of the game, the promise, the overcoming of the logic of bullying, could I think be seen as a realization of this.

I often say that in terms of organizing direct actions, well, there's endless literature on the mob or "the madness of crowds", and most people do assume that any kind of crowd is necessarily going to be, collectively, stupider than any one of the individuals that make it up. That's why most people accept the legitimacy of authoritarian leadership. If this were really true, it stands to reason that if you took even any one random person out of the crowd and made that person dictator, the crowd would make better decisions than it would as as a collectivity. Anarchism is about the possibility of a crowd becoming smarter—not just than any randomly selected member of it—but of any individual member of it. It's about creating those modes of communication and deliberation which would allow that to happen. Hence the emphasis on practice.

So in that sense, dialogue is your primary build-ing-block. It's a form of emergence of thoughts that no individual would have been able to have by themselves, which is ultimately what anarchy too is about—which is why I don't think it so crazy for this conversation to take the four-way form that it did. No?

Well, I was hoping it might.